D0867763

Homelessness in the Classroom

Teaching Our Most Vulnerable Students

Kerri J. Tobin and Brandy S. Gros

ISBN 978-1-64504-194-8 (Paperback)

ISBN 978-1-64504-195-5 (Hardback)

ISBN 978-1-64504-196-2 (E-Book)

Library of Congress Control Number: 2021944767

Printed on acid-free paper

This book is part of *Curriculum: For Curriculum by Curriculum*

Series Editor: Kenneth J. Varner

Table of Contents

Introduction

A record high 1.5 million children in the United States experienced homelessness last year (National Center for Homeless Education, 2020), a number that skyrocketed during the 2007-08 recession and has remained troublingly high. With Covid-related evictions looming on the horizon as we write in spring 2021, this number is unfortunately expected to get even higher.

Homelessness is nothing any child should have to experience. It is at best unpleasant, at worst highly traumatizing, while it is happening, and can have lingering effects even after a family finds housing. Having been homeless portends negative educational outcomes like lower test scores and lower high school graduation rates than those of stably-housed children. Homelessness in childhood is also linked to entry into the juvenile justice system. The majority of people who suffered homelessness as children say that it had lifelong effects on their ability to feel safe and secure, their mental health, and their sense of self. What's worst, perhaps, is that childhood homelessness predicts adult homelessness.

How did we get here? Child homelessness was largely eradicated in the United States after the Great Depression, but owing to a series of choices made at the federal policy level, family homelessness made a re-emergence in the 1980s. Since then, researchers have tried to understand the problem of family homelessness, its causes, and its impacts on families with children. One thing we can say for sure is that, though the specific experience is different for every family, housing instability is not good for children.

Although most people agree that children experiencing homelessness are a vulnerable population in need of support, there are some researchers who contend that because we cannot be sure that homelessness has greater effects on children's schooling than the already well-known negative impacts of poverty and high mobility, studying homeless children as a group may deflect attention from the pressing needs of all low-income students. On the other hand, there are those who believe that the comparison is irrelevant: homeless children are worthy of attention in and of themselves. Taking a position that borrows from both stances, we believe that supporting homeless children's needs at school stands to benefit *all* children.

There are decades of research about this population of children and their families, and much has been discovered, but "student homelessness remains an invisible and extremely disruptive problem" (Ingram et al., 2016, p. 4). One glaring omission has been the role and experience of the classroom teacher in the education of children without stable housing. Policymakers and researchers seem to forget how much power teachers have, possibly because most school systems seem to curtail teachers' power as much as possible. Prescribed, even scripted, curricula; emphasis on logging minutes of instructional time; the monotonous and ever-present drudgery of test preparation – these seem designed to ensure that teachers do not have a chance to put their own individual stamp on the profession. John Dewey would be aghast. But despite decades-long attempts to strip them of their autonomy, teachers absolutely can and do make their classrooms their own. Policymakers and administrators may be where ideas and rules originate, but these things simply cannot happen without cooperation from teachers. Teachers are the people who translate policy into practice, who follow or break the rules, who meet needs the leaders haven't even identified yet, who figure out how to do what needs to be done. Teachers are the front line in meeting the needs of unhoused children.

Collectively, we have spent over two decades attempting to fill gaps in what is known about homelessness and education. This volume represents our best effort to bring teachers what we know about how to support this specific group of learners. Perhaps because Kerri was a teacher in New York City before she became a researcher, and she recalls quite clearly how unprepared she felt to meet the needs of students who lived at the shelter a few blocks away from PS 25X, the classroom has always seemed to her to be where our attention ought to be focused. We also have no doubt there are teachers all over the country employing best practices for these students that researchers have yet to discover.

This book is organized in the way we think is most likely to be useful to K-12 classroom teachers. It begins with an introduction to the concept of "homelessness" in Chapter 1, with some probing to get at the deeper concepts and policy issues involved. Next, we present the last four decades of research: Chapter 2 presents what researchers have discovered about how homelessness affects children's experiences with schooling, while Chapter 3 explores what the research has uncovered about the best ways to teach undomiciled students in our classrooms. In Chapter 4, we look at how to help graduating seniors prepare for the next stage of their lives without family support. Chapter 5 explores a somewhat newer area that has taken hold of the field of education in recent years: trauma and its impacts on children. The experience of trauma is not unique to children who experience homelessness, but it is more common among them. Chapter 6 explores what teachers can do to support students in their classrooms, and Chapter 7 attends to the issue of compassion fatigue: what it is, how it affects teachers whose students experience homelessness, and how to avoid it in hopes of being the most effective teachers we can be. We finish in Chapter 8 by sharing our thoughts on how to move forward with the work of supporting students who are unhoused.

A note on terminology: researchers and advocates in this field generally prefer to use person-first language, e.g., "people experiencing homelessness," "children who are not housed," rather than the essentializing / stigmatizing "homeless children" or "the homeless," as the latter seem to strip the subjects of their humanity, if only accidentally. The latter terms also imply a permanence to homelessness that is not accurate. Most families will experience only a short episode or episodes when they are without housing. Homelessness, for most, is not a permanent state of existence. Likewise, the term is imprecise since, as we will see in Chapter 1, being without a *house* does not necessarily mean someone is without a *home*. We feel strongly that a crucial aspect of educating for social justice lies in recognizing the full humanity of people in challenging circumstances. However, in the interest of space, efficiency, and fluidity of prose, we do sometimes employ the terms "homeless," "undomiciled," or "houseless" in front of "students" throughout this work. Most local, state, and federal policies use the word "homeless" as well, so we use that when what we write explains or mirrors such legislation.

Chapter 1

What is homelessness?

With a million and a half children experiencing homelessness, schools need to be aware of and responsive to their needs. But before we can even begin to think about the impacts of homelessness at school, we have to start with a very simple question. What, exactly, is homelessness? Perhaps you're thinking that this is a simple question (and wondering whether you've made the right choice in opening this book), but with closer examination, it becomes quite complex. On the surface, if we just take the word apart, homelessness means being without a home. But what, exactly, is a home? Is it simply a roof over one's head? A roof and walls? A roof, walls, and electricity? Electricity and heat? Running water? A place to store food? A place to prepare food? A place to sleep? What about physical security or emotional support?

For many of us, the word *home* conjures up much more than a roof and walls – home is where our family is located, a place where all our low- to mid-level Maslow's hierarchy needs (Fig. 1) are (more or less) met, hopefully even a place where we feel safe and accepted. Though there are many adaptations of Maslow's (1954) model of human needs circulating in academic and popular circles, it is interesting to note that they differ on where to put *shelter*: some versions place it at the bottom, in the most essential category of physiological needs, but others list it in the second tier, a facet of safety and security.

Figure 1: Maslow's Hierarchy of Needs (1954), adapted

This ambiguity of the placement of *shelter* in the hierarchy reifies the philosophical nature of the question of what homelessness really means. Is *home* a place that provides food and water? Or a place that provides safety and security? Need it be both? What happens if it is one but not the other?

Still another confusing consideration in defining homelessness is that most of us can conjure up an image of a perfectly sturdy structure – a house – safe from the weather and any outside intrusions, with all the amenities of modern living, where the inhabitants are cruel to each other and where love and belonging do not exist. We know that there are luxury homes inside which children are not physically safe. Are these structures still *homes*? On the flip side, can a loving, intact family who've lost their house and are residing in their car be at *home*? At the urging of people experiencing it, advocates and journalists (e.g., Vespa, 2020) are starting to adopt the word "houseless" to replace "homeless," exactly because the physical structure might be completely apart from the emotional experience of having a home.

We list these considerations to get readers thinking about what *home* really is and what purpose it serves primarily as metaphysical exercise, but there is also a very practical reason to engage these questions and decide on a definition of the word *homeless*: to determine who does and does not qualify for public housing assistance. Regardless of exactly what any of us think government should look like, it has to use clear definitions to draw lines around populations in order to distribute our collective resources. This task proves difficult for homelessness. The main agencies tasked with providing support to homeless families, the Department of Housing and Urban Development (HUD) and the Department of Education, use different definitions.

When teaching undergrad and graduate students about homelessness for the last decade, Kerri often begins the discussion by asking the class to imagine a fictional student, Cathy, who has just finished her junior year of college. She tells them a made-up story about how Cathy and her roommate live in an apartment off campus. But this fictional apartment has a roach infestation and the landlord won't do anything about it[1], so they decide to move when their lease is up on May 31st.

They find a new apartment, but the lease does not begin until August 1st. So, Kerri asks the students, will Cathy be homeless in June and July? They invariably say no, of course not – she can go home to stay with her parents. Well, her parents are dead, Kerri tells them, and she doesn't have any other family. Okay, they respond, she can crash with friends, it's only a couple of months. Nope. Cathy's an introvert and doesn't have any friends other than her roommate, who's off to live in Europe with her own parents for the summer. Cathy can't afford a plane ticket, so she can't go stay with them. Is she homeless now?

Students still lean toward no. Cathy is young, educated, and should be able to figure out a solution for herself. So Kerri adds another wrinkle: Cathy has to work to pay tuition for the one summer class she has to take (she got bad advising and missed a class she needs to graduate, so she has to take it this summer – unfortunately, students can almost always relate to this part of the scenario). It seems our fictional Cathy really has to stay put. Well, she can get another job, the students reply, and stay at a hotel. We calculate the price for this and always find it to be out of reach for someone working at minimum wage. But they're still hesitant to say Cathy should qualify for any kind of government assistance, because of 1) the length of time she'll be without shelter combined with 2) what we assume to be some constellation of skills and supports Cathy must have, which might be called her cultural capital (Bourdieu, 1973). Basically, we believe that if Cathy has gotten to college, she must have some way to provide for herself now.

Some students will suggest that Cathy forego the summer class and graduate late. But what if she has a scholarship that ends after four years, Kerri asks them, and missing this one class will mean she cannot graduate? Do we want two months of summer housing to be the reason she enters the workforce and adulthood without a degree, knowing what we know about the positive relationship between a college degree and future earnings (Abel & Deitz, 2014)? Usually, the class splits at this point: some go toward personal responsibility – she shouldn't have relied on the advisor who told her to take the wrong class, saddling her with the summer class, and she should suffer the consequences. Nothing is irreversible, they say, she'll just have to delay graduation and work full-time next year. The other half of the class generally starts to wonder aloud whether, for moral or even practical purposes, it wouldn't make more sense just to invest in Cathy's housing now, because her college degree will make her much less likely to suffer poverty (and require government assistance) in the future.

As the class grapples with the dissent among their ranks, Kerri throws in the final challenge: what if Cathy has a child? This makes everyone pause. The half of the class that was already leaning toward giving her housing support is generally pushed totally in that direction by this final detail. To them, the benefits to fictional Cathy, her hypothetical toddler, and society as a whole obviously outweigh whatever it will cost the government to provide her housing benefits for two months so she can finish college on time. The personal responsibility crowd generally also finds their position solidified by this news, though in the opposite direction – Cathy's child is the proof they needed that Cathy is irresponsible and doesn't deserve any help from anyone. Kerri reminds them we have no idea how Cathy came to be with child, and delivers a sobering talk about the prevalence of sexual assault, but the personal responsibility group is still unconvinced. The class usually arrives at an impasse.

3

This exercise seems silly to people who haven't yet started to study homelessness in any depth. Cathy's fictional case seems hyperbolic, a ridiculous set of challenges that would never actually all happen to the same person. This is the worst-case scenario, students say. Most people don't end up homeless because of such compounded bad luck.

Or do they?

As we will read in Chapter 5, people who experience homelessness are much more likely than those who are housed to have been victims of domestic violence (Aratani, 2009), sexual abuse, or assault (Portwood et al., 2015). Indeed, 80% of children in one study had witnessed a violent act either in their own family or in their neighborhood (Swick, 2008). We will learn more about childhood adversity in Chapter 5, but for now it's important to note that having experienced multiple traumas in childhood is linked to homelessness later in life (Koegel et al., 1995). Homeless adults are also likely to have experienced homelessness during their own childhoods (Parpouchi et al., 2021). We are starting to understand that homelessness is often the end product of a long line of unlucky and even victimizing events (Masten et al., 1997). The role of trauma – experiences whose emotional and physical impacts on the body last well after the danger has passed – is newly being understood for its role in homelessness as well as a whole range of other negative life outcomes (Centers for Disease Control, CDC, 2019). Homeless mothers generally find themselves unsheltered or in emergency housing only after having exhausted all of their social capital. In other words, they have stayed with friends and family until no options remained (Shinn, 2009). It turns out that homelessness, far from a result of personal failure, exists at the far end of a spectrum of bad outcomes produced by a host of system failures – lack of affordable housing (Watson et al., 2017), insufficient or unavailable care for mental health and substance dependence (Hallett & Skrla, 2017), racial employment discrimination (Fryer et al., 2013), inadequate welfare programs (Tobin & Murphy, 2012), and even educational inequity.

But while there is much to be said about how people find themselves without shelter, that is not the focus of this book, so we need to return to the original question of this chapter: how do policymakers and program leaders decide who is homeless so they can provide assistance and possibly try to understand these people and their needs as a group? The United States government provides some guidance here, but even within it there is confusion. Almost inconceivably, different agencies use different definitions.

The United States Department of Housing and Urban Development (HUD) has traditionally defined as homeless "an individual who lacks a fixed, regular, and adequate nighttime residence" who resides in a "supervised publicly or privately operated shelter designed to provide temporary living accommodations" or "a public or private place not designed for, or ordinarily used as, a regular sleeping accommodation for human beings" (HUD, 2010). For these purposes, "fixed" means the residence does not change every night and that it remains in one place; "regular" means the accommodation can be used nightly; and "adequate" means "meets the physical and psychological needs that would be expected within a typical home environment" (Hallett & Skrla, 2017, p. 32). People classified as homeless under this definition might be sleeping in cars or on park benches and sidewalks, or living in temporary/emergency shelters provided by their municipalities or local non-profits (see Appendix A). This fits the image most people in the US have in their heads when they think of the word "homeless."

The United States Department of Education, however, defines homelessness differently. It uses the definition in the McKinney-Vento Homeless Assistance Act of 1987 (42 USC 11302), which starts out including all the same people as the HUD definition, but in a major departure, also includes children in families forced to share accommodation with others due to financial hardship (See Appendix A for exact wording). These families are commonly referred to as "doubled up," and in the case of youth, "couch surfing," and if they are counted, the number of homeless people in the US more than doubles (Mykyta & Macartney, 2011). Almost three quarters of students experiencing homelessness are doubled up (Hallett & Skrla, 2017).

This difference in definitions means that if two families have to share a home intended for one family (whether they are related or not), the adults in the family are not considered homeless, are not counted in any official statistics, and do not qualify for housing assistance, but the children in those same families, when they come to school, are considered homeless and qualify for protections under the McKinney-Vento Act. Using its more-narrow definition, HUD only officially counts somewhere in the vicinity of 550,000 homeless individuals most years (e.g., Henry et al., 2017), but this number is contested by advocates and many researchers. And whatever its size, somewhere between 35% and 50% of the homeless population in the US are children living with their families (Barnes et al., 2019). Additionally, some young people experience homelessness without their families. These are generally teenagers who have been kicked out of or have run away from the family home. The National Council of State Legislatures (2019) reports that about 700,000 such minors, called *unaccompanied youth*, experience homelessness each year. These young people are exceptionally vulnerable. They generally choose to leave home because of abuse, and those who are told to leave home often become unwelcome when their parents discover their LGBTQ+ identity or an unintended pregnancy.

In 2009, the Obama administration passed the Homeless Emergency Assistance and Rapid Transition to Housing (HEARTH) Act in response to the mortgage crisis and resultant recession of 2007. The HEARTH Act amended and revised the McKinney-Vento Act, making some important changes (see HUD Exchange, 2020 for more information). Advocates lobbied to convince the administration to use this opportunity to make the HUD and Department of Education definitions match, to include doubled-up individuals and families in the group deserving of housing assistance, to no avail. The only apparent concession that appears in the bill is the creation of an "at-risk" group: a family or individual that is doubled up but will lose even that housing in fewer than 14 days can be considered at risk of homelessness and given certain types of housing assistance (Morton et al., 2017). Regardless of exact definitions, however, we know that "homelessness comprises a range of living conditions that impinge on children's abilities to cope with their daily reality, including school" (Shields & Warke, 2010, p. 790).

I think that a lot of times people think that homeless is staying under a bridge or someone that doesn't have anywhere to go, but a lot of our students are doubled up, which means they're living with another family. Or sometimes the parents are in prison, so they have to live, or in jail or wherever, or abandoned them, and so the students are living with their grandparents. That's also considered homeless…a lot of families [live] in hotels or motels… So homeless under the education term is kind of broad. Whereas, homeless, you know, in our state of mind, we think "nowhere to go."

-Jennifer, homeless education administrator

An additional complication in the work of understanding the scope and severity of student homelessness is that researchers have started to examine the similarities between students who are technically homeless and those who may never go without a roof over their heads but are considered "highly-mobile," meaning they change residences more than once during a single school year. Multiple studies have found that when we expand the definition this way, often referring to this larger group of students as H/HM, for "homeless/highly-mobile" (see, e.g., Obradovic et al., 2009; Tobin, 2016), we find that outcomes are very similar for both groups. It may be that the experience of moving, of changing living situations (and sometimes schools) is a leading cause of academic challenge for both these groups. So while HUD concerns itself solely with people who do not have a roof over their heads, the Department of Education uses McKinney-Vento's definition and includes children who are living in doubled-up situations, and researchers have found evidence that even moving often, without technically losing housing, can cause students to fall behind in school.

Urgent needs

Homelessness is not something that usually happens out of the blue, and it tends to bring other instabilities with it. Although many middle-class families found themselves without homes during the foreclosure crisis of 2007-2008, homelessness is still primarily a condition that results from poverty and any number of complicating factors. Foundational researchers Rafferty and Shinn describe family homelessness as "a composite of many conditions and events, such as poverty, changes in residence, schools, and services, loss of possessions, disruption in social networks, and exposure to extreme hardships" (1991, p. 1170). In addition, prospects for homeless students are very bleak if they do not succeed in traditional ways at school. Lack of education can have long-term effects on employment and social integration (Obradovic et al., 2009; Powers & Jaklitsch, 1993). Research has demonstrated repeatedly that the returns to education are high and increase as more education is attained, meaning that education helps with life outcomes like finding stable employment and being able to afford shelter, food, and medical care, and the more education a young person completes, the more likely they are to secure a stable adulthood. It is very important that we figure out how to support unstably housed children in school, lest "the educational deficits that homeless youth develop [become] serious economic, social, and health handicaps" that affect them as adults (Shane, 1996, p. 32), which is unfortunately common (Ingram et al., 2016).

However they are defined, whether using the HUD or McKinney-Vento definitions or the ones developed by researchers, unstably housed children need support to thrive once they get to school. The experience of homelessness will be described in greater detail in Chapter 2, but it is important to know that the ways homelessness manifests in the classroom are many. They are best understood when grouped together into the following categories: physical health, mental health, and academic outcomes. Schools have a vital role to play in first identifying these students so they can be connected with the services to which they are entitled under the McKinney-Vento Act, and then ensuring those services are delivered.

Physical health

Children experiencing homelessness are more likely than their housed peers to suffer from infestations, infections (Hudson et al., 2010), and asthma (Sakai-Bizmark et al., 2019). Many children without homes also experience hunger and malnutrition (Lippert & Lee, 2020). Malnutrition is particularly problematic because without proper nourishment, children's brain development can be stunted. Hunger has a devastating impact on children (Weinreb et al., 2002), affecting their growth and physical health, potentially leading to mental health and behavior problems (Rafferty & Shinn, 1991). Though few studies have tracked the long-term health implications of childhood homelessness (Gultekin et al., 2020), malnutrition brings the potential for life-long learning issues (National Center on Family Homelessness, 2009). And teachers understand all too well that children who are not adequately nourished and who are often ill may miss school and, when they do attend, find it difficult to pay attention to what is going on in the classroom (Hart-Shegos, 1999).

Mental health

Although housed children from low-SES backgrounds may also experience mental health issues at above-average rates, children experiencing homelessness are likely to exhibit behavioral difficulties, increased levels of anxiety and depression (D'Sa et al., 2020), and suicidality (Barnes et al., 2019). In short, the most troubled children in our classrooms are the ones we need to look at most closely. We know that children don't choose to misbehave any more than adults choose to be anxious or depressed, so when we see challenging behaviors in children, we need to look deeper. We will discuss this further in Chapter 5.

Academic outcomes

Unfortunately, children who do not have stable housing also have lower test scores (Tobin, 2016), and are more likely to leave school without graduating (Masten et al., 2015). Although the physical and mental health challenges that often accompany homelessness may contribute to these academic outcomes, the most consequential link identified in the literature is attendance (e.g., Fantuzzo et al., 2102; Tobin, 2016). Children experiencing homelessness are seven times more likely to miss school than their housed peers (Nolan et al., 2013), and this is often directly correlated with lower scores and grades. In Chapter 6, we will talk about ways that schools and teachers can try to support attendance for children experiencing homelessness.

Identification

Conflicting definitions from different stakeholders can make it difficult to identify who should receive housing-related support and from which agencies. And confusion over who is homeless and who is not doesn't stop with policymakers. Educators and parents alike are unsure who qualifies (Hallett & Skrla, 2017). Although every school district is required to have a homeless education liaison, sometimes even liaisons do not know exactly what homeless students need (Hernandez Jozefowicz-Simbeni & Israel, 2006). What's more, McKinney-Vento provisions have never been adequately funded (Wong, et al., 2009).

> I think we do the best we can with the funding that we have. Um, we do provide them with uniforms, school supplies, assistance with enrolling in school. Um, so we're doing the best we can with what we have...there's a great need, and the money doesn't match the need.

> *-Jennifer, homeless education administrator*

This means schools sometimes have an incentive not to notice who is homeless, because funding to support them is not available. Getting students the services to which they are entitled continues to be a challenge, but some areas have made important strides, and we now understand that identifying which students are without housing is the crucial first step – "in order to address the needs of homeless children, one must know whether a child is experiencing homelessness" (Canfield, 2015, p. 103). We will talk more about this important task in Chapter 3, but first we will examine what homelessness looks like in a school context.

Notes

1. It is often news to students that tenants have very few rights in most states. They want some mechanism to force the landlord to fix the infestation, but the truth is that in many states and cities, no such process exists. Or if it does, it is expensive and time-consuming. Many major cities do not have tenants' rights organizations (see, e.g., Desmond, 2017).

Chapter 2

How does homelessness manifest in school?

[O]n top of the absenteeism, children would be physically tired and mentally exhausted because they couldn't really process what they were doing on a day-to-day basis…stress because they didn't know where they were going that afternoon. They didn't know if they were getting on a bus or getting in a car or walking or who would be there to pick them up.

-Harper, first grade teacher

Their main issue was focusing, because if they're hungry, they can't really concentrate, or if they had to find a place to sleep, they were very tired in class.

-Robin, high school teacher

As noted in the last chapter, homelessness can lead to a lot of negative outcomes for children. The problems facing this population are "compounded by the lack of awareness of the issue in many communities" (Ingram et a., 2016, p. 4). Many teachers are not aware of their students' housing status or of the McKinney-Vento Act that mandates that homeless students receive specific types of supports at school. Though it is not commonly seen, researchers have known of the problem of student homelessness for decades and have learned some valuable lessons about what these students experience. But not all homelessness is the same. Three traditional forms are well-known, and another form is starting to gain attention. Understanding these forms helps broaden the complexity of what homelessness looks like in an educational setting. The first form of homelessness is *episodic*: episodic homelessness is when a person is currently experiencing homelessness and has had at least three periods (or episodes) of homelessness in the last year. The second form is *chronic*: chronic homeless is four or more episodes of homelessness in a year (National Coalition for the Homeless, 2021). These two forms are the more common and known forms of homelessness. These individuals may struggle with mental illness, a physical disability or be dually diagnosed with both and mental and physical disability. The third form of homelessness is *transitional*: transitional homelessness happens when a person is going through a major life-changing event, like sudden loss of a job, and then becomes homeless. The fourth and newly-added form is *hidden*: hidden homeless happens when an individual is doubled up without immediate prospects for permanent housing. Hidden homelessness exists when people are staying in the residences of relatives or friends (Unite, 2019). These two forms, transitional and hidden, are the most common in education. Doubling up or living with other families made up 76.7% of homeless children and youth enrolled in public schools for the school year 2018-2019 (NCHE, 2021). Regardless of form, homelessness and many of its challenges overlap with issues we might also see from other vulnerable groups, such as academic struggles, mental health instabilities, and even physical health challenges. Getting students identified and then connected with services to support them is crucial, so we need to know what the profile of a homeless learner might look like in school.

Academic signs

Homeless elementary school children experience academic problems such as low test scores, low grades, and high rates of grade retention. Masten and team's (1997) study looked at standardized test scores, teacher ratings, and cumulative school records of 73 homeless children in Minneapolis and concluded that they experienced substantial academic delays at rates well above national norms. Likewise, an examination of school data showed that 156 homeless children in and around Boston had greater rates of school failure than national norms (Bassuk & Rubin, 1987). Researchers are generally in agreement that homeless children are more likely than their middle-class peers to score low on tests, and to be held back and made to repeat a grade.

Though homeless children have been shown consistently to experience greater academic problems than middle class children, the first researchers to examine this issue had difficulty determining if they also fared worse than never-homeless children from low socioeconomic status (SES) backgrounds. "[T]he absence of a comparison group of poor housed children [was] a common methodological problem in studies" of this type (Zima et al., 1997, p. 239) and "few studies... compared homeless children with youngsters from a comparable SES background who live in homes, [so] it is not clear what interventions are specifically needed to help homeless children, as opposed to poor children in general" (Rescorla et al., 1991, pp. 211-212). Some more recent studies have begun to employ control groups of low-SES children, but evidence from these studies is mixed.

Test scores

Most studies of homeless children's academic outcomes rely on standardized tests, such as those administered by states and cities to school students, and/or IQ tests of the sort usually administered to individual children by psychologists. Homeless children consistently score below norms on standardized tests, and often worse than their housed low-income peers. Results on IQ tests are less straightforward, but troubling nonetheless.

Standardized tests. Studies of standardized test scores over the years across the country have found homeless children's scores well below city, state, and national norms. In perhaps the most sophisticated study, Rubin and colleagues (1996) performed multivariate analysis to compare 102 homeless children with 178 housed children from the same classrooms in New York City and found that homeless children performed significantly worse on tests of reading, spelling, and math. The large sample size and use of a classroom-based control group improved internal validity of the study. Using this matching technique controls for classroom, teacher, and school effects, increasing the likelihood that housing status was what linked students and lower scores. Though their sample size was smaller, Shinn and colleagues (2008) conducted a rigorous longitudinal study and found that, compared to a never-homeless control group, students in the midst of an episode of homelessness scored one third of a standard deviation lower on tests, a finding that was statistically significant. But Buckner, Bassuk, and Weinreb (2001) studied children in 220 homeless and 216 low-income housed (never homeless) single-parent families in Worcester, Massachusetts, and found no significant differences between the academic scores of homeless and housed poor students once attendance had been controlled for.

Less sophisticated studies have turned up similar results. In one of the first studies of New York City, only 42% of homeless children were found to perform at or above grade level on the Degrees of Reading Power test, compared with a citywide pass rate of 68%; results on the Metropolitan Achievement Test of mathematics were similarly disparate, with 28% of homeless children scoring at or above grade level, while 57% of children were at grade level citywide (Rafferty & Rollins, 1989). Rafferty (1990) examined test scores of 9659 homeless school-aged children in New York City and found that they had significantly lower scores not only than citywide averages, but also lower than the average scores of the 73 schools with that served the largest low-income student populations. Results from studies like these have remained consistent for decades. Fewer than half of all students experiencing homelessness in the state of Florida achieved proficiency on math or reading tests in 2013-14 (Tobin, 2015). In that same year, only 20% of homeless third through eighth graders in New York City scored at or above grade level on state math assessments, and only 16% did so on English language arts tests (Institute for Child Poverty and Homelessness, 2016). Figure 2 shows that according to federal data, in the last decade or so, unhoused students have lagged behind national norms on both math and reading proficiency by between 19 and 22%.

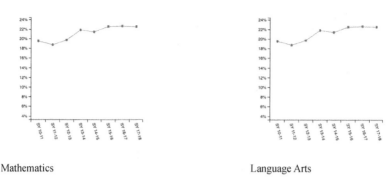

Mathematics   Language Arts

Figure 2: Proficiency gap between all students and homeless students, 2010-2018

Source: United States Department of Education Data Dashboard, 2021

IQ. Could homelessness even impact a child's IQ? One of the earliest studies of the educational scores of homeless children was undertaken by the St. Louis Children's Project in the 1980s. Researchers administered the Slosson Intelligence Test – Revised to 107 homeless children and found that 45% of them – three times the proportion of the overall population – scored in the borderline/"slow learner" category. The Peabody Picture Vocabulary Test–Revised yielded similar results: 89% of the children fell at or below the 50th percentile (Whitman et al., 1987).

Unfortunately, while pointing to lower average IQ scores for homeless children than national norms, this work did not offer the opportunity for comparison with housed extremely poor children. The most recent and rigorous studies have not found any differences in IQ score between homeless and housed low-income children. Rubin and colleagues (1996) found that homeless students and the housed low-SES classroom comparison group had equivalent scores on verbal and non-verbal IQ tests, as did Shinn and her team (2008).

In their study of 83 children living in 13 shelters across Philadelphia, Rescorla and team (1991) used a housed low-SES comparison group and determined that the school-aged homeless children scored significantly lower on the Weschler Intelligence Scale for Children (WISC) vocabulary test, which measures knowledge gained as a result of environmental experience. However, the comparison group of housed poor children was half the size of the homeless group, and the sampling method was problematic. Housed poor families were recruited at a local health clinic, introducing potential bias. Some unobserved family factor may influence both children's IQ score and the parents' propensity to seek health care at a clinic. These issues make this study less reliable than those finding no differences in IQ between housed and houseless low-income children.

While we can't say for sure what the relationship is between IQ and homelessness, we do know that for adults, living in poverty is correlated with lower scores on measurements of cognition, equivalent to 13 points on an IQ test (Kelly, 2013). A pair of studies conducted in the US and India administered cognitive assessments to participants, then measured their scores after they'd been exposed to financial hardship, and found that they scored lower on the second administration of the same tests. Something about the stress of poverty, the researchers concluded, impeded the participants' cognitive function (Mani et al., 2013). Researchers have also found links between stress and smaller hippocampal volume (Piccolo &

Noble, 2018), which is itself linked to poorer cognition (Pohlack et al., 2014). The hippocampus is the part of the brain responsible for learning and memory. These findings about poverty and decreased cognition are so compelling that a groundbreaking multi-site research study was launched in 2018 to measure and track children's brain function when parents are given monthly cash payments to alleviate their financial woes (Baby's First Years, 2021). This longitudinal study also tracks parents' stress by measuring their cortisol at various points in the year. The results are still forthcoming, but the study aims to determine more about exactly how poverty leads to the learning challenges other researchers have already discovered. We will learn more about the possible connections between poverty, stress, and academic achievement in Chapter 5.

Performance

I found out he was homeless from him. He actually told me, after a while that his grades had been falling. [I]t was around the flood. He [told] me he lost pretty much everything in his home, he didn't have family around, so they were living out of a motel…when they could afford it but when they couldn't afford it, they would pretty much be on the street.

-Stephanie, middle school teacher

School performance is another area in which homeless children fare worse than middle-class children and, in some cases, even worse their housed low-SES peers. What is performance, exactly? It is measured slightly differently from study to study. Some researchers have used parent reports of students' grades, others use teacher reports, and still others look at nebulously defined "grade levels" as measures of school performance. Although Rafferty, Shinn, and Weitzman (2004) found no differences in homeless and housed low-income students' academic scores before the former group's homelessness or five years after their re-housing, they did find that students' scores dropped below the control group's during the episode of homelessness. So it is possible that the effect of homelessness on children's school performance dissipates after the child is back in stable housing. Hart-Shegos (1999) reviewed literature and concluded that three quarters of homeless children performed below grade level in reading and half performed below grade level in mathematics.

Though they rely on parent or teacher report rather than more objective measures, some other studies support the same conclusions. Maza and Hall (1990) studied 340 children in 163 families served by Traveler's Aid (homeless assistance) agencies in eight major cities and found that 30% were reported by their parents as being behind grade level in school. Whether those children were truly behind academically or were simply held back a grade because of too many absences is hard to determine. Bassuk and Rosenberg (1990) studied families in six Boston shelters along with a housed low-income control group and found that 41% of homeless mothers reported that their children were failing in school, compared with only 23% of the housed comparison group. Ziesemer and colleagues (1994) found no significant differences between 169 homeless and 167 highly mobile housed low-SES students in Madison, Wisconsin on measures of academic functioning based on teacher reports.

As we noted in our introduction, a lot of early research energy went into trying to determine whether homelessness was "worse" for children than poverty. Since we already have decades of research showing that all low-SES children do worse on measures of academic attainment than higher-SES children, and most children who experience homelessness already come from low-SES backgrounds, some researchers hypothesized that looking at housing status was redundant. We take the position here that it is nonetheless important to try to parse out differences between the groups, and to search for approaches that could work for both groups. This approach has proven effective in other areas of education. For example, Maria Montessori developed her signature preschool system specifically for children with cognitive disabilities, but it turns out to be an effective approach for all children. Likewise, if we can isolate classroom activities and teacher behaviors targeted at homeless student success, we might find interventions that improve education for all students.

Retention

Studies of homeless children have generally found that they are more likely than other children to repeat a grade in school (NCFH, 2009), sometimes dramatically so. Rafferty (1990) found that homeless students in New York City had a rate of retention (15%) more than twice that of the city average (7%). Rubin and colleagues' (1996) study of 102 homeless children in the Bronx and Manhattan comparing them to a classroom-based control group of 178 housed children determined that the homeless children were 4.8 times more likely to have repeated a grade than their housed classmates. Hart-Shegos (1999) postulated that this often happens for non-academic reasons like absenteeism and mobility, rather than failure to meet particular learning goals. It is worth noting that early studies of retention took place before No Child Left Behind made standardized testing high-stakes. It is reasonable to imagine that retention numbers have gone up quite a bit since then, both across the board and for undomiciled children specifically. As pressure on schools has mounted, retention is one tool they have used to try to boost test scores. Some researchers now estimate that over the course of the academic careers, 50% of homeless children will be made to repeat a grade once, while 22% will be retained more than once (Ingram et al., 2016).

Other obstacles

Mobility – frequent changes in residence and school – is common for homeless children and seems to place them at a distinct academic disadvantage. Increased suspensions from school and special education needs coupled with low rates of receipt of special education services also create obstacles to homeless children's academic performance.

Mobility

Homeless and housed low-SES children are likely to experience higher rates of residential and school mobility than middle-class children (Evans et al., 2010).

Whether it is a marker of risk or an actual cause of problems, mobility is very common in houseless children (Nuñez & Collignon, 1997). In one study, 41% of undomiciled children had attended two schools in the same year, and 28% attended three or more (Hart-Shegos, 1999). Dworksy (2008) studied homeless children in Chicago and discovered that they had changed schools an average of three times per year, with 60% of these changes taking place mid-year. Masten and colleagues (1993) found that homeless children in their studies were more likely than housed extremely poor children to have changed schools. In a New York City study, the previously homeless children had experienced more school mobility in the five years after they were re-housed than the never-homeless low-SES comparison group (Shinn et al., 2008).

Whether it means just changing residences or also changing schools, moving frequently is associated with problems in school (Lubell & Brennan, 2007). Even when moves are expected and desired, they involve tumult and transition for children and adults alike. Something as simple as learning where the light switches are in a new residence can make people feel disoriented when they find a new place to live. Children are often affected by changes in residence, especially when those changes require them to downsize their belongings and part with treasured items. The disruptiveness of moving is exacerbated when families have to double up; more people in cramped spaces means more opportunity for discord.

Mobility also causes problems by interrupting schooling processes. "School transfers result in discontinuous instruction that requires remedial instruction to address academic deficits" (Powers & Jaklitsch, 1993, p. 402). The National Center for Homeless Education (2006) posits that a student can lose months of learning with every change in school, particularly abrupt or unexpected moves in the middle of the school year. Moves may also temporarily increase absences, already a problem for children experiencing homelessness: Rafferty and Rollins (1989) found that the children in their study missed an average of five days of school every time they changed shelters. The negative effects of moving appear to be worse for elementary school students than those in upper grades (Hart-Shegos, 1999).

In their 2001 review, Scanlon and Devine found that residential mobility was negatively associated with academic performance; Jelleyman and Spencer (2008) found that moving was correlated with behavioral problems as well. Particularly if changes happen mid-year (Samuels et al., 2010), school mobility has negative effects on achievement (Duffield et al., 2007; Dworsky, 2008). However, studies comparing student outcomes before, during, and after moves (Buckner et al, 2001; Heinlein & Shinn, 2000) have not found a direct link between school mobility and changes in academic test scores: "school mobility…may be a marker of a constellation of adverse conditions rather than an independent cause of poor outcomes" (Samuels et al., 2010). Mobility is linked to low test scores in many studies of homeless children.

Rubin and colleagues (1996) reported that the effect of housing status on reading test scores was mediated by the number of school changes a child had experienced in the previous two years. Buckner and colleagues (2001) determined for their sample that having changed schools frequently was a greater predictor of school outcomes than housing status. Some scholars have suggested that mobility is so disruptive that it may be more appropriate to examine homeless and highly mobile children together, comparing them to stably-housed low-income children. One longitudinal study of homeless and highly-mobile children in Minneapolis found that as a group, these students evidenced greater educational risk over time than housed poor children. "Among socio-economically disadvantaged children, compelling data suggest that homeless and highly mobile (H/HM) children fall at the high end along a continuum of risk for academic problems and related psychopathology" (Obradovic et al., 2009, p. 493).

Suspensions

Because they cause students to miss class time and because they are indicative of behavioral issues that may cause ongoing interference with instructional delivery, school suspensions are an additional hypothesized link between homeless children and their academic outcomes. Buckner and colleagues (2001) found that more homeless children (22%) in their Worcester, MA sample had been suspended from school than their low-income housed peers (13%). A study of children in supportive family housing across the Minneapolis metropolitan area found that 28% of children ages five to eleven and 52% of children ages 11 to 18 had been suspended from school (Gewirtz et al., 2008). The Better Homes Fund (1999) found that twice as many homeless children had been suspended from school than housed children.

Special education

Homeless children qualify for special education services at school at up to twice the national average (Gargiulo, 2006; NCFH, 2009). Nuñez (1994a) reported that homeless children were more than three times more likely than their housed peers to be referred for special education services. Dworksy (2008) found that 22% of the homeless children in her Chicago study were identified as needing special education intervention. Endres and Cicade (2015) also found that rates of special education were higher for unhoused students than national norms. One quarter of the homeless children in Bassuk's Boston study were in special education classes (as cited in Molnar et al., 1990). In Rubin and team's (1996) study, 8% of the homeless children were enrolled in special education classes, compared with only 1% of the housed comparison group. Unfortunately, a seminal study (Duffield et al., 2007) found that while undomiciled children were more likely than the general population to qualify for special education services, they were also concurrently less likely to be receiving those services at school (see also Buckner et al., 2001; National Center on Family Homelessness, 2009).

Zima and colleagues (1997) examined the need for special education evaluation of 169 homeless children in Los Angeles and found that the children in their study were four times more likely to have symptoms of a behavior disorder, three times more likely to exhibit a learning disability, and eight times more likely have mental retardation than the general population of school-aged children. Unfortunately, though 45% of the school-aged homeless children in their study merited a special education evaluation, only 23% of those with a disability had ever received special education testing or been in special education classes (Zima et al., 1997). This disconnect between need and services may be caused by the lengthy special education referral process, which commonly takes between three and four months – students with high school mobility may not be with the same teachers long enough to have their needs identified and evaluated (Emerson & Lovitt, 2003). The length of the special education referral process "run[s] counter to the immediate service needs of homeless students" (Stronge, 1993, p. 344). Students' high mobility is a challenge not only for them, but for teachers and school administrators as well (Eddowes, 1993), possibly causing the latter to be wary of investing the time and resources for special education evaluation in children likely to leave the school before it is complete. In 2004, the reauthorization of the Individuals with Disabilities Act (IDEA) included language about expediting the special education evaluation process for students experiencing homelessness, but many districts still do not have appropriate processes in place (Bowman et al., 2008). Expedited evaluations are nonetheless strongly recommended for these children to prevent gaps in service delivery (Santos, 2017).

Though this book is meant to provide research-based information for practitioners, we sometimes feel it's important to include anecdotal support for what the research shows. We have worked with and taught children who were residing in emergency shelter and those who were doubled up. In the most extreme case, Kerri had a second-grade student, we'll call her Jessica, whose recorded address was the emergency homeless shelter closest to the school. Students who resided there came to school on a bus, which arrived and left earlier than the other students every day (which created a stigmatizing situation in itself), so in Jessica's case, identification was not a challenge. She also came to school every day in the same uniform shirt. If she got a stain on it, that stain would be visible all week. She also didn't always smell very clean, which didn't lead to a great deal of success in peer relationships. Jessica also struggled mightily with academics. She was eight years old (most second graders are seven, so this indicated that she'd been retained, though we had no proof because she showed up to school that year with no records from her previous school and we were never able to obtain them). Not only could she neither read nor write, she couldn't consistently put the letters of the alphabet in order. When Kerri asked the administration at school if they could refer Jessica for a special education evaluation, she was told "those kids" never stay long, so it wouldn't be worth the time.

Jessica stayed the entire year. Kerri ended up doing a clothing drive among her own family and friends and making anonymous drop-offs at the shelter for her. She also kept a pair of sneakers in the classroom closet so Jessica would always be able to participate in gym class. And of course Kerri kept food in her desk, as so many teachers do, and would slip her something subtly so she would have food to take out at snack time. So many teachers go to lengths like these, and they're not too burdensome when only one or two kids have this level of need. But as part of her dissertation research many years later, Kerri interviewed teachers in high-poverty schools who reported that kids who experience homeless don't even stand out because all the students have such dire need. Teachers' own pocketbooks are not the answer when half of public school children in the United States live near or below the poverty level (Koball & Jiang, 2018; National Center for Education Statistics, 2020a). And these efforts do not often solve academic struggles: because she never got any intervention, Jessica could order the letters of the alphabet by the end of second grade, but literacy was still a long way away for her.

Mental Health

Since the earliest studies of homeless children, researchers have employed nationally-normed diagnostic tools to measure homeless children's mental health: the Child Depression Inventory (CDI), the Child Behavior Checklist (CBCL), and the Diagnostic Interview Schedule for Children (DISC), which allows for formal classification using the Diagnostic and Statistical Manual of Mental Disorders (DSM), are commonly used. Although the nature of some of these measurement tools complicates drawing conclusions about mental health conditions (Rafferty & Shinn, 1991), homeless children are believed to experience some mental health problem more frequently than middle-class children and, in some cases, than their housed low-SES peers (Lubell et al., 2007). This is to be expected, since "the environments of homeless children are uniquely chaotic, marked by frequent moves, family structure changes, household and neighborhood disorder, parenting distress, and lack of continuous services" (Marcal, 2017, p. 349).

Although mental health issues have long been noted in children from low-SES backgrounds (Aber et al., 1997), anxiety and depression have been found in unhoused children at rates much higher than national norms (Molnar et al., 1990). One review found that a third of homeless children have at least one mental health problem that interferes with daily activities and nearly half (47%) have problems with anxiety, depression, or withdrawal, compared to 18% of other school-age children (Hart-Shegos, 1999, p. 8). Additionally, homeless children may suffer greater behavior challenges in the classroom (Masten et al., 1997) and more stress (Buckner et al., 1999), which we will explore in greater detail in Chapter 5.

Anxiety and depression

Researchers regularly report that homeless children suffer more mental health issues than middle-class children generally do. Their mothers suffer more, as well, than housed mothers (Bassuk & Beardslee, 2014), and maternal mental health impacts children's mental health. There is also an established link between maternal depression and homelessness (Curtis et al., 2014). Bassuk and Rubin (1987) were among the first researchers to detail the mental health and emotional challenges faced by homeless children. When they administered the CDI to the school-aged homeless children in their study, they found that more than 50% scored above the cutoff for psychiatric referral, and a majority of children answered, "I think about killing myself but I would not do it" to a question regarding suicide (Bassuk & Rubin, 1987, p. 8). For homeless teens, homelessness is associated with a fourfold increase in suicidal ideation (Beharry, 2012). Further tests indicated that the homeless children in the study had greater anxiety than national norms. Schmitz, Wagner, and Menke (1995) found that the homeless children in their study had high anxiety, and that grade point average was impacted by it. Furthermore, they stated, "the most direct relationship existed between anxiety and current domicile status. Consistent with findings from previous studies homeless children exhibited higher levels of anxiety" (Schmitz et al., 1995, p. 313). Unfortunately, studies have also found that although they are more likely than middle-class children to have mental health issues, homeless children are unlikely to receive professional mental health treatment (Bassuk & Rubin, 1987; Better Homes Fund, 1999) and even when they do, it has low levels of success (Marcal, 2017).

Homeless students have been shown in some studies to suffer greater mental health challenges than housed poor children as well, but results are inconclusive. The CBCL relies on parent or teacher reports of child behavior to assess children's mental health, introducing several problems. Teachers and parents each use their own subjective lenses to view children's behavior, and children may behave differently in and out of school. Rescorla and colleagues (1991) used the parent version and found higher rates of emotional maladjustment in homeless school-aged children than the housed clinic-drawn sample. It is important to note the small size of their samples, however, with the comparison group of 45 barely half the size of the homeless group. Ziesemer, Marcoux, and Marwell (1994) used the teacher version of the CBCL and found no significant differences between the 142 housed and 145 homeless children in their study. Shinn and colleagues' (2008) study of 388 children between birth and age 17 found that the homeless children had significantly more mental health problems than the comparison group of housed poor children only in the four- to ten-year-old age range.

As previously noted, the effects of family homelessness are not limited to children, and impaired parental mental health may affect students' school outcomes. Boxhill and Beaty (1990) found that living in a shelter or hotel negatively affected parent-child relations. Bassuk and Rubin (1987) note that the homeless mothers in their sample also evidenced higher rates of mental health issues than the general population, concluding that "the data describing the homeless mothers and the children suggest an intergenerational cycle of family disruption and emotional difficulties" (p. 284). Sustained parental depression has been shown to have negative consequences for homeless children (Molnar et al., 1990). Hart-Shegos (1999) expounds on this link between mothers' and children's mental health by explaining the role of anxiety and worry in the lives of homeless children, who "worry about their families: their parents, whose stress and tension is often shared with the children, and their siblings, for whom they see themselves as primary care givers" (p. 7). It is not hard to imagine how these worries might interfere with concentration at school.

Behavior

In addition to diagnosable conditions like depression and anxiety, many homeless children also suffer from non-clinical behavior issues that may impact their classroom experiences. "Teachers have reported listless, apathetic, and tearful behavior" (Gewirtzman & Fodor, 1987, p. 241). Based on structured diagnostic interviews, Yu and colleagues (2008) found that the 157 homeless children in their study had more disruptive behavior problems than the 61 housed children. Internalizing (e.g., withdrawal) and externalizing (e.g., aggression) behavior problems may be up to four times more likely in homeless children than national norms (Zima et al., 1997). Children in Bassuk and Rubin's (1987) study in Boston demonstrated more behavior issues than the general population on the Simmons Behavior Checklist, such as sleep problems, shyness, withdrawal, and acting out. They also indicated low frustration tolerance, with only 37% of the children in the study manifesting age-appropriate responses to challenging tasks (Bassuk & Rubin, 1987). These behavioral problems can interfere with students' readiness to learn and can lead to higher incidence of removal from the classroom for disciplinary reasons. One study suggests that behavior problems may be worse when children first enter the shelter, but get better over time (Samuels, Shinn, & Buckner, 2010).

Explanations for these behavioral challenges generally point to the increased exposure to stressful events and lessened social ties that characterize homelessness. The ways in which homeless children's social ties suffer is under-studied, but we can speculate. Homeless children's relationships with parents may be prone to deterioration due to stress and role confusion. They may also have lessened ties to peers because of frequent moves and emotional responses to stress that put strain on friendships. Houseless children may actively distance themselves from making new friends because they've been hurt by losing old friends when they moved, but they nonetheless feel a strong desire for social acceptance (Begg et al., 2017). Likewise, homelessness can bring stigma that prevents children from being accepted by their peers. Masten's team (1993) noted that the homeless children in their study were significantly more likely to have experienced friendship disruption than the housed comparison group, which the researchers expected to have an impact on psychosocial functioning, particularly increased social isolation. They found that academic scores were related to behavior and adaptive functioning in the classroom in their study; behavior and academic problems co-occurred (Masten et al., 1997).

Some studies, however, do not find that homeless children experience more behavioral problems than their low-SES peers. Buckner and colleagues (1999) found that homelessness was initially associated with internalizing problems, but after three to four months, the effect tapered off. They hypothesized that children may, over time, acclimate to homelessness and unpleasant shelter conditions. Housing status was not associated with externalizing problems in the children they studied, but they acknowledge the weakness of using a shelter-based sample: many shelters turn away children who have behavior problems, possibly leading to selection bias that obscures the real incidence of these issues in homeless children (Buckner et al., 1999), and leaving those children and their families even more vulnerable and without help.

Although Ziesemer and her team (1994) found homeless students in Madison, Wisconsin, had higher rates of behavioral problems than a national sample of low-SES children, with one quarter of the homeless students having enough behavioral problems to warrant further assessment and an additional 10% with scores indicating "severe behavioral deviance" (p. 663), homelessness was not identified as the only predictive factor. Their team made strides to improve the comparison group by looking at 145 sheltered homeless children and 142 low-SES children who also experienced high residential mobility, and found no differences in behavior or adaptive functioning drawn from teacher responses on the CBCL between the two groups (Ziesemer et al., 1994). Buckner and his team (1999) also found that residential instability did not predict behavior problems, concluding that unstably housed children might get used to frequent moves and be less affected by moving than children who previously had stable housing.

Physical Health

There are a couple of signals that when you get to know you students, whether it's somebody who had a lot of energy and they come in very tired the next day, or vice versa. One girl in particular, it was her clothes…she had always come in so perfect every day, hair perfect…and she came in a few days in a row and her clothes were tousled and wrinkled and soiled…I asked her 'what's going on?' and she said she didn't have a place to stay, like she'd been sleeping at different people's houses.

-Erin, high school teacher

Most school-age children suffer acute infections and illnesses, but homeless children are more likely to have these types of minor medical issues, as well as more serious chronic health problems, and to fall ill more often (Grant et al., 2007b). The National Health Care for the Homeless Project studied 19 major U.S. cities and found homeless children twice as likely as a national sample to be treated for respiratory and ear infections, three times as likely to be treated for gastrointestinal issues, four times as likely to suffer skin problems, and ten times as likely to have dental problems (Molnar et al., 1990). The same project discovered that homeless children were almost twice as likely as the national sample to suffer chronic health problems like cardiac disease and neurological disorders, and these results are supported by smaller studies in Seattle and New York City (Alperstein, Rappaport, & Flanigan, 1988; Molnar et al., 1990). Mihaly (1991) reported that homeless children had twice the rate of asthma of other poor children. More recent studies (Grant et al, 2007a) find that homeless children still suffer extremely high rates of asthma, and are 31 times more likely than housed children to be hospitalized for asthma treatment (Sakai-Bizmark et al., 2019). Hospitalizations present a clear challenge to school attendance and may result in loss of learning.

Because they have difficulty accessing health care and health insurance (Chatterjee et al., 2019), homeless children's minor health issues often become serious and take more time away from school. Likewise, homeless children are three to four times less likely than their housed low-SES counterparts to be immunized on schedule, leaving them vulnerable to more serious illnesses (Acker, et al., 1987). In addition, research has shown that homeless children have higher exposure to lead than housed low-income children (Alperstein, et al., 1988), and lead exposure has been linked to cognitive and behavior problems (Marshall et al., 2020). Both chronic and acute illness can impact children's school performance by causing absences. And even when they are in class, physically ill children can reasonably be expected to experience listlessness, withdrawn behavior, and exhaustion, none of which is conducive to learning (Powers & Jaklitsch, 1993).

In addition to the above-noted health challenges, homeless children are likely to suffer from hunger and malnutrition (Gultekin et al., 2020) often because shelters lack cooking facilities, forcing parents to resort to fast food or junk food, which does not provide necessary nutrients (Molnar et al., 1990). Homeless families are likely to experience food insecurity that leads to hunger: more than a third of homeless children report having to skip meals (NCFH, 2009). One fifth of homeless parents interviewed in a Los Angeles study said that they were forced to let their children go hungry because of lack of food, compared with 4% of housed low-SES parents, and 21% of the homeless parents reported they had been unable to feed their children sufficiently at least four days in the previous month (Mihaly, 1991). Although many homeless children and their families qualify for federal nutrition assistance like the Supplemental Nutrition Assistance Program, up to half of those eligible for the programs may not actually receive the benefits (Kiesler, 1991). School breakfast programs have been shown to have a positive effect on short-term memory and some learning skills, as well as on attendance (Cueto, 2001), but school meal programs provide only breakfast and lunch, not dinner, and do not provide meals on weekends or school holidays. In one study of children in Worcester, MA, researchers found that hunger was common among school-aged homeless children and linked to illness and anxiety (Weinreb et al., 2002).

Like hunger, malnutrition is dangerous. It can lead to stunted growth, iron and other mineral deficiencies, and other "lifelong repercussions" (Molnar et al., 1990, p. 111), including negative effects on students' learning (Olson, 1999). Alaimo, Olson, and Frongillo (2001) showed that, even controlling for other confounding poverty-related variables, math scores were significantly lower among elementary-school children with food insecurity, and these children were also more likely to have repeated a grade. Owing to food security and other health challenges, homeless children are likely to be tired, sick, or hungry and have trouble concentrating and completing classroom tasks. These make it difficult for them to develop new knowledge and skills (Hart-Shegos, 1999). Without these skills and content knowledge, students' scores predictably drop. Furthermore, homeless children suffering malnutrition and lead poisoning may suffer lasting cognitive damage (Gordon, 2003) that can hurt academic performance.

Conclusions

Homelessness is very difficult for adults and children both. Unstable living situations, frequent moves and changes of not only home but also school can throw children's lives into chaos. Hunger and malnutrition, increased health challenges, stress, and the emotional experiences that accompany homelessness affect everything from academic performance to mental and physical health. In the next chapter, we will examine best ways for meeting the needs of these very vulnerable young people.

Chapter 3

Are there best practices for teaching undomiciled students?

Reading about the topic of homelessness in children can be overwhelming. Teachers rarely experience it as uplifting. But there is good news: schools can help. Schools can make the experience less traumatic as it is happening, and they can set children up for success in the future. In this chapter, we outline some of the ways in which schools can meet the needs of their unhoused or unstably housed students.

There is a great deal of literature promoting the enormous potential of schools to "provide developmental havens of safety, stability, and care for children living in poverty whose lives are complicated by homelessness or residential instability" (Masten et al., 1997, pp. 43-44). The National Association for the Education of Homeless Children and Youth (2010) asserts that "school is a refuge for homeless children...providing safety, structure, and services" (p. 2). Early researchers Zima and team noted, "the structured environment of a school program fosters the child's concept of personal place and may be a main source of stability for a homeless child." (Zima et al., 1997, p. 236). Although "schools cannot be expected to address the societal level economic and socio-cultural problems that may underlie" homelessness, they can be part of the solution (Masten et al., 1997, p. 43).

Homeless children themselves also see a positive role for school in their lives. Early on, Horowitz and colleagues (1988) compared homeless and housed children in the same classes and found that the homeless children were more likely to express positive feelings toward school. "Findings from this study suggest that [homeless] children, given the extremely stressful events surrounding their home life, maintain a positive attitude toward school...the school environment may function in facilitating [their] adaptation" (Horowitz et al., 1988, p. 36). Some youth even verbalize that that schools are the most stable aspect of their lives (Hallett & Skrla, 2017).

Likewise, Ziesemer and team (1994) found that that the homeless children in their study had "a strong belief in the value of academics and good behavior" (p. 666), leading researchers to conclude that "one of the clearest social policy implications of [our] research is of a pressing need for children who are homeless to be enrolled in a stable and supportive school program" (Rescorla et al., 1991, p. 219). The McKinney-Vento Act was passed in 1987 to make school accessible to children experiencing homelessness, but we also know that they still struggle even in 2021 not only to gain access, but to achieve success once they get there. What they need are teachers who understand their challenges but focus on their strengths to get them on the path to academic success. Begg et al. (2017) found that although the third through sixth graders that they interviewed struggled to imagine safe and secure futures for themselves, they believed very strongly in their own need to do well in school in order to have at least some chance at stability in adult life. Even more than their housed peers, children who have experienced homelessness have a profound understanding of what is at stake and what can be lost, or never gained, if they are not able to achieve success at school. Knowing this, it is imperative for us as educators to make school into the safe and supportive place it can be. Scholars generally issue a call to action along the lines of that stated by Masten, et al. (1997): "while additional research is necessary, schools can use the knowledge that has accumulated to develop and evaluate programs to foster educational success in these children" (p. 43).

First things first: Identification

Before they can deliver appropriate services, schools have to identify who is homeless. The McKinney-Vento Act (Appendix B) has made this a priority for schools since 1987, but many teachers have never heard of the Act and have no idea about their students' housing statuses. One third of district homeless liaisons report that they are the only personnel in their districts who receive any training about how to identify unhoused students, and almost 10% say there is no training in their districts for anyone at all (Ingram et al., 2016). A majority of teachers in our own research state the same. Most staff are not knowledgeable about the definitions or the signs of homelessness in children. Making sure that we as teachers not only remember these definitions but also try to raise awareness in our colleagues can go a long way. Once teachers know what they're looking for, they can become crucial partners in the task of getting student homelessness noticed.

> When you open up the definition like that then you would find quite a few. I mean, I have had so many students who talk to me about, "Yeah, I don't stay with my mom or dad. I stay with my aunt or even my older sister or cousin." You know, there's certainly a lot of, uh…I think moving from family member to family member for various reasons that occur.

-Matthew, 7th grade teacher

Another group of people whose awareness needs raising is parents themselves. Because they may only be familiar with the HUD definition, parents who are doubled up may have no idea that their children are considered homeless at school. And even when they do know, many parents are hesitant to report their homelessness to the school (Tierney & Hallett, 2012; Tobin, 2011). This reluctance is sometimes rooted in shame; parents are often embarrassed to admit they have lost their housing, feeling they will be judged or that their children will be stigmatized.

What's worse, some municipalities remove children from their families and place them in foster care simply because their parents have lost housing (Institute for Children, Poverty, & Homelessness, 2017). Parents have legitimate reasons for withholding their housing status from school personnel, and this is something practitioners have to contend with.

Front office personnel are often the first people parents and guardians come into contact with when they register children for school. Sensitivity and awareness trainings for these important school employees can help them ask the right questions and support parents to trust the school with sensitive information (Williams & Korinek, 2000). Another way for schools to identify children experiencing homelessness is for teachers to be aware of how their challenges manifest in the classroom (Tobin, 2011). Signs that children may be experiencing homelessness (Gargulio, 2006) include:

- Chronic absenteeism/frequent tardiness
- Inconsistent personal hygiene
- Habitual tiredness in school
- Complaints of hunger, evidence of hoarding food
- Lack of school supplies
- Inadequate/inappropriate school apparel
- Incomplete homework assignments
- Reluctance or inability to provide address or telephone number
- Unresponsive parent/guardian (notes from school go unsigned, for example)
- Unwillingness to go home after school

This list is not exhaustive, nor does it provide definitive proof of anything about a child's housing situation, but teachers on the lookout for signs like these are more likely to notice if a child is undomiciled (or otherwise in need of intervention). Academic, physical, and mental health challenges can be signs to look out for as well.

> I think there's a lot of kids that are flying under the radar and don't get found out… who may just sleep on a couch, on the floor, maybe not even a blanket to sleep with on the floor that we don't know about because our plate was so full and we were so stressed out as teachers.

-Erin, high school teacher

As we write in spring 2021, a return to in-person schooling looks promising for the fall, but there are no guarantees. Students experiencing homelessness have an additional set of challenges when trying to access virtual school. Some signs to look for in a virtual environment include:

- Frequent changes in the background of where the student is working
- Many different people in the background
- Background appears to be a public area, outdoors, or motel/hotel
- Student or parent is unreachable for periods of time

- Student is unwilling to turn on their camera
- Inconsistent internet access

(SchoolHouse Connection, 2021)

Teachers have a lot of tasks, and it can feel burdensome to add another to the list, but the stakes are extremely high for this student population.

After identification

They just want to be treated like anybody else.

-Robin, high school teacher

A wealth of literature exists to recommend ways in which schools can help undomiciled students. It is by and large comprised of advocacy and single case-study research, lacking evidence we generally want to see before we can promote specific practices (Mawhinney-Rhoads & Stahler, 2006), but it is what we have and we can make suggestions based upon it. In the absence of a rigorous evidence base, we can still make recommendations based on what has worked in small-scale situations and what we know about students experiencing hardships in general: they cannot learn if they don't feel safe and cared about at school (Aupperle et al., 2012).

Researchers and advocates have compiled a relatively consistent set of recommendations for schools to use in supporting the social and academic learning of homeless students (Murphy & Tobin, 2011). Effective interventions range from those legally required by the McKinney-Vento Act, which are detailed in the next section and include removing transportation and documentation barriers, to those hypothesized to improve service delivery and facilitate academic and emotional success. These can be divided into the four main categories of removing logistical and procedural barriers, meeting children's physical needs, promoting homeless children's mental health, and addressing their specific learning readiness challenges.

Removing barriers: The McKinney-Vento Homeless Assistance Act of 1987

Homeless children have historically faced logistical and procedural barriers to schooling. They have long been denied the right to enroll in school because of missing documentation like immunization records and proof of residence (Stronge, 1993). Additionally, homeless students face issues with transportation to and from school. Although its name has changed slightly throughout its re-authorizations, the aims of The McKinney-Vento Homeless Assistance Act (PL100-77), signed into law by Ronald Reagan on July 22, 1987, have remained consistent. Subtitle B, the Education for Homeless Children and Youth (EHCY) program, laid out guidelines for states to ensure children have "access to a free, appropriate public education which would be provided to the children of a resident of a State" (sec. 721[1]). Title VII deals with the education of homeless children and youth.

McKinney-Vento was updated by the 2016 Every Student Succeeds Act

(ESSA), but at its core, it remains the same. The law specifies that homeless children have a right to be educated with their classmates, not segregated in special classes or programs (Funkhouser et al., 2002). It also makes clear that districts have a responsibility to make efforts to identify homeless children so they can receive the services for which they are eligible (Stronge, 1993) and to make information available to children and parents about the rights of homeless children in school (PL100-77; Samuels et al., 2010). It creates a system of district and state education agency coordinators responsible for the planning and execution of delivery of services, including the required appointment of a homeless education liaison in every school district nationwide, and provides funding structures. ESSA also expanded the law cover summer school, preschool, and extracurricular activities (Hallett & Skrla, 2017).

Personnel. Although the law requires that each Local Educational Agency (LEA), known to most people as a district, appoint a liaison for homeless education, this person does not have to have only that job. Nine out of ten liaisons work in another official capacity for their districts (Ingram et al., 2016), most often working as the Title I coordinator as well. Most liaisons are able to dedicate only about 2 hours per week to homeless student issues because they have so many other responsibilities (Government Accountability Office, 2014). And researchers have even found that in some cases, liaisons do not even know they hold the title (Jozefowicz-Simbeni & Israel, 2006). So while creation of the position is a step in the right direction, this clearly does not guarantee that services will reach students.

The right to enroll. Even once they are identified, children experiencing homelessness face challenges getting to school and even being allowed to enroll. The law is clear that they must be allowed to enroll, but advocates and liaisons repeatedly report challenges in this area.

> A lot of times students face barriers with enrollment...a lot of times the schools don't want to enroll them because they don't know how many credits they have. So our office advocates for them to go ahead and enroll the child...get him a schedule...get him going...and then find out the rest of the stuff on the back end.

> - *Jennifer, District Liaison*

In the past, houseless families often had difficulty producing the documents necessary to enroll children in school, such as birth certificates, immunization histories, and records from previous schools (Mihaly, 1991). McKinney-Vento attempts to deal with these issues, giving students the right to be enrolled while parents make arrangements to locate documents. There is evidence that this barrier has been significantly reduced though not eliminated (Samuels et al., 2010).

Many homeless students have also been prohibited from enrolling in school without proof of permanent residence or guardianship (National Coalition for the Homeless, 1987). Although the McKinney-Vento Act requires districts to allow students to enroll without such evidence, adherence to the law has not been quick or universal. In 1991, Mihaly documented that 30 of the 50 states still used illegal residency requirements. And there is some suggestion that these problems persisted even two decades later – for example, in the fall of 2009, four students in Pennsylvania were denied access to their school when they lost their home and stayed in a shelter outside the district (Pennsylvania Legal Aid, 2010) – though their extent is difficult to gauge. Most research finds that the McKinney-Vento legislation largely achieved its goal of increasing homeless students' ability to enroll in school (Stronge, 1993). Masten and colleagues (1997) looked at the educational outcomes of 73 children in a Minneapolis shelter between the ages of 6 and 11 and found that enrolling in school was not a problem. Stronge (1993) asserts that by the early 1990s, homeless students nationwide had begun to attend school at rates similar to the general student population, and a national evaluation of the Education for Homeless Children and Youth program found that over 85% of homeless students were attending school regularly (Anderson et al., 1995).

The McKinney-Vento Act requires states to "review and undertake steps to revise...laws" to ensure that homeless children are able to enroll in school (sec. 721[2]). Specifically, it requires states to determine whether it is in the child's best interest to remain in the district where they attended school before losing housing (the district "of origin"), or to be transferred to the district where they currently reside (sec. 722[e][A][B]). The law also stipulates that guardianship requirements be made flexible for students as well, since children placed with family or friends while parents enter the shelter system may not have guardians available to enroll them in school (National Coalition for the Homeless, 1987).

McKinney-Vento has been reauthorized several times, each time expanding the scope and strengthening the provisions of the original legislation (National Coalition for the Homeless, 2006). The amendments have specified more clearly how districts should prevent procedural barriers from impeding homeless students' enrollment. Such paperwork requirements as immunization records, birth certificates, or previous school records (Swick & Bailey, 2004) are required to be made flexible; students can enroll immediately even without them (Tierney, Gupton, & Hallett, 2008). In the 1994 amendments, parents and students were given a voice in school placements (National Coalition for the Homeless, 2006). In cases where families and schools disagree about whether the school of origin or the school where a student is currently residing is the best choice, the school the family prefers must enroll the student while the dispute is resolved and if the two schools are in different districts, the two districts must determine between them how transportation will be provided for the student (James & Lopez, 2003).

Transportation. Transportation has long been the most significant logistical barrier to enrollment documented by homeless education analysts (Rafferty, 1990). In 1982, educational leaders in 22 states identified transportation as the major reason for homeless children's absences (Mihaly, 1991). The National Center for Homeless Education reported in 2009 that Local Educational Agencies continued to identify transportation as the number one problem for homeless students (as cited in Samuels et al., 2010).

The McKinney-Vento Act requires that school districts provide transportation for homeless children to and from school (Samuels et al., 2010). This includes cases where a student stays in a shelter outside the district but remaining in their school of origin is found to be in their best interest. In such cases, school districts must provide transportation across district lines. Unfortunately, McKinney-Vento has been underfunded since the beginning, so provision of such transportation can be problematic. In a 1995 evaluation of the Education for Homeless Children and Youth program, researchers concluded that "state coordinators and local school district administrators have worked hard, with limited resources, to ensure homeless children's and youth's access to a free, appropriate education" (National Coalition for the Homeless, 2006, pp. 5-6) but that the resources allocated to the McKinney-Vento programs are insufficient to meet demand, and that lack of adequate funding limits the programs' success (Anderson et al., 1995).

In 2010, the National Association for the Education of Homeless Children and Youth reported that homeless education liaisons still report transportation to school of origin as a major barrier confronting homeless children. In 2018, several students, represented by a public interest law firm, sued the Missouri state board of education and a St. Louis-area school district for "refusing or delaying necessary transportation to [homeless] students," e.g., when one of the plaintiffs in the suit "moved…it took nearly a month for transportation to be arranged, even with the assistance of a legal advocate," and the student was not able to attend school (Scott C., et al. v Riverview Gardents, 2018). They settled in 2020, with the district agreeing to use the recommendations of a homeless education expert to help them follow McKinney Vento law (Patrick, 2020). We also cannot discount the role of stigma or shame in keeping students at home.

> He told me, you know, he didn't want all the kids to know about this, but he lives in a homeless shelter. And I sort of got to know him a bit on a personal level, his family and him. And I sort of took him under my wing, and…I would bring him home after school [but]…he told me he didn't want me to drop him off at the homeless shelter because he didn't want [anyone] to see that environment.

-Morgan, 6th grade teacher

Even if they can enroll and do have transportation, homeless students may have problems with excessive absence for other reasons. They may be reluctant to attend because they lack proper clothing (Gewirtzman & Fodor, 1987) and school supplies or because they have been stigmatized by classmates and even teachers unaware of their circumstances (Gewirtzman & Fodor, 1987). Parents may opt to keep children home from school to protect them from another temporary experience, or for fear of being located by an abusive partner (Mihaly, 1991). Other researchers suggest that the chaotic experience of homelessness itself sometimes prevents parents from being able to focus on getting students to school consistently (Nuñez & Collignon, 1997).

Because of these continued problems getting to school once they are enrolled, homeless children still have attendance problems. Zima and colleagues (1997) studied 118 families with 169 children in shelters in Los Angeles and found that although the majority were enrolled in school, 39% had missed more than a week of school in the preceding three months. In a review of research from across the country, Molnar, Rath, and Klein (1990) found that attendance was poor, with only between 43% and 57% of homeless children attending school regularly. Rafferty and Rollins (1989) found that, in New York City, not only did homeless children have worse attendance rates than city averages, but that their attendance got worse as they got older at a higher rate than for children overall. Rubin and colleagues (1996) found, similarly, that the homeless students in their study missed significantly more days of school than the students in the housed classroom-based comparison group. More recent studies have found that this trend continues (The Road Map Project, 2015). Harpaz-Rotem, Rosenheck, and Desai (2006) found that maternal homelessness was associated with lower attendance in school. In some studies, homeless children's absences have been tested for their relationship to academic problems (e.g., Tobin, 2016). "Days absent from school was hypothesized as the mediating link between homelessness and academic achievement" (Buckner, et al., 2001, p. 45).

Meeting physical needs

Many researchers have pointed out how physical issues, both health problems and access to physical resources like food, clothing, and school supplies (Medcalf, 2008; Swick, 2008), interfere with homeless children's attendance, learning, and school success. These scholars point to the role of the school in ensuring that children's basic physical needs are met (Nuñez & Collignon, 1997). "If education is to be meaningful in their lives and in the lives of their families, basic human physical…needs must be addressed" (Stronge, 1993, p. 355). First and foremost, schools can provide basic school supplies like backpacks, notebooks, and pencils (Delmore, 2004). Second, schools can see to it that students have access to clean and appropriate clothing, without which students may fear social ostracism (Penuel & Davey, 1998). Some schools even make these supplies available to all children so as to remove the stigma associated with homelessness (Yon et al., 1993) – and because they recognize that housed low-income children may also have trouble accessing basic amenities (Gonzalez, 1990). In 2016-2017, the Whirlpool corporation partnered with Teach for America to identify schools where students would benefit from having facilities at school to wash and dry their clothes. The program initially donated machines to schools in Los Angeles, Chicago, Atlanta, and New Orleans to see whether clean clothes could improve student attendance, and based on their findings, ultimately increased its scope to include over 100 schools (Keagy, 2020).

Transportation assistance. Schools may also need to provide transportation assistance, above and beyond what is required by the McKinney-Vento Act. If students are given passes for riding public transportation, for example, schools can ensure that students are shown how to read local transit maps and know how to get from school to home and back (Delmore, 2004). They can be assigned a buddy who rides the same route or gets on/off transit at the same stops. Parents, too, need to be oriented to the transportation so they can help support their children's school attendance (Hart-Shegos, 1999). And schools need to make common sense decisions about how to make transportation known. At the first school where Kerri taught, students who resided at the nearby shelter were provided with transportation on a school bus, and 20 minutes before the end of every school day, an administrator would get on the PA system and make an announcement to the whole school: "All the children who ride the bus to the shelter, line up now." It should be obvious to anyone who works with children that having their homelessness thrust into the spotlight like this, day after day, was emotionally difficult for students. We can understand how something like this might even make students less likely to come to school at all. On the flip side, some districts arrange school bus transportation such that the shelter is the first stop in the morning and the last stop in the afternoon, so no other children are on the bus to see who gets on and off there. Understanding that there are many parts of providing transportation, and taking steps to ensure that the process preserves student dignity, is a crucial part of getting kids to school.

Food. Food insecurity is often a significant issue for homeless children (Quint, 1994). Homeless students have a demonstrated need to participate in free breakfast and lunch programs at school. Students can be enrolled without filling out paperwork (Duffield et al., 2007) and are expected to be given access to these programs immediately (Delmore, 2004). Teachers can also make snacks available in the classroom (Reed-Victor, Popp, & Myers, 2003), and most do. Additionally, parents should be provided with information about how they can get food for themselves and their families either on site at the school or through connections with community programs (Hart-Shegos, 1999). Food banks and school districts across the nation have long been forced to devise ways to send enough food home with students on Friday to last the weekend (Greene, 2010), and during the Covid-19 school shutdown, with how to deliver meals at all (Centers for Disease Control and Prevention, 2021). Children also need food during school breaks and over the summer. Some municipalities provide lunch or dinner (or both) at public libraries or other community locations. Teachers would do well to familiarize themselves with these programs so they can share the information with students, parents, and other school staff.

Medical services. Physical health, the one arena where research nearly conclusively finds that homeless children are worse off not only than middle-class children but also their housed low-SES peers (Buckner, 2008), is also thought to be a mediating factor between homelessness and school success. The physical maladies that plague homeless children are well documented (e.g., Books, 2004; Grant et al., 2007b; NCFH, 2009) and are believed to stem from lack of access to acute and preventative health care as well as unhealthy conditions in some shelters and other temporary living situations (Gultekin et al., 2020).

Because homeless children are likely to be behind on immunizations and often lack needed health services, scholars have long recommended that schools take immediate steps to screen and immunize them (Hart-Shegos, 1999). Some schools provide clinic hours on site for children and have a school nurse review medical issues with children and parents on the first day of school (Gonzalez, 1990). Gewirtzman and Fodor (1987) pointed out that schools have greater access to children than community organizations and so have the potential to deliver health services quickly and effectively. Homeless teens are also likely to need access to reproductive health care because rates of sexually transmitted infection are much higher in homeless unaccompanied youth than in housed adolescents (Beharry, 2012). These youth benefit from school-based health clinics and school personnel who are familiar with health resources in the community.

Promoting mental health

Students experiencing homelessness are, as previous sections have shown, likely to be experiencing mental health problems. Either because they have familial stresses common to low-SES children but often occurring more frequently in homeless families, or because the very experience of losing one's home and being forced to relocate is traumatic, these students have emotional needs that scholars agree must be met by schools. As Stronge (1993) notes, "educators may not be able to bring into focus academic goals for [homeless] students until pressing social and psychological needs have been addressed" (p. 345). Gonzalez (1990) concurs: "the psychological needs of the children…are as important as their instructional needs because these children suffer the combined effects of poverty, anxiety, and depression" (p. 787). Additionally, homeless students' academic work also suffers when their emotional needs are not prioritized. In Chapter 5, we will go into greater detail about ways that the classroom can be responsive to undomiciled students' emotional needs.

Sensitizing school staff. Perhaps the most prevalent recommendation for schools found in the literature on supporting homeless students is the provision of training for teachers and other school personnel on the needs and challenges of students in this position (Williams & Korinek, 2000). As Gewirtzman and Fodor asserted back in 1987, "the first step in working with these children is understanding the conditions in which they live" (p. 242).

> Sometimes the sensitivity of some staff isn't there… the schools sometimes make it hard on the parent, without realizing that that parent is homeless and the parent doesn't want to divulge all that information in the front office.

-Jennifer, Homeless Education Administrator

Because they have the most interaction with students, teachers are the focus of recommendations for sensitivity training (Nuñez & Collignon, 1997). "[T]eachers can play a crucial role in providing a safe and secure learning environment. By educating their colleagues about the issues of homelessness, informed teachers… minimize the ostracism and pressures experienced by homeless students" (Powers & Jaklitsch, 1993, p. 406). However, researchers note that all the adults in a school building can benefit from gaining understanding of the issues homeless children face (Morris & Butt, 2003).

> I wish there could've been more resources because it wasn't talked about at all at the school. Not during team meetings which were mandatory, weekly. We didn't have any resources mentioned in professional development meetings, just nothing. I've actually been homeless myself, bounced around from home to home when I was younger…that's pretty much the only training that I have. There should at least be a one-in-a-year seminar…they spend thousands of dollars for some speaker, that could talk about [homelessness], but that's not done.

-Stephanie, middle school teacher (3 different schools in 2 districts)

Most see this sensitization taking place in professional development or other training provided by school social workers or counselors, though Stronge and Hudson's (1999) study recommended that "awareness-raising activities" might be more broadly construed (p. 10), including training on how to recognize the signs that indicate a student may be experiencing homelessness (Duffield et al., 2007; Gargiulo, 2006). Some principals go to extraordinary lengths, like taking new teachers to visit the local homeless shelter at 6am, so they can see exactly what their students' lives look like before school. Housed students, likewise, stand to benefit from education about the issues their homeless classmates face (Noll & Watkins, 2003); some researchers (e.g., Nuñez) have gone so far as to publish children's picture books about homelessness for use in the elementary school classroom. Ziesemer and colleagues (1994) recommend that social workers conduct education and sensitivity training for teachers and students around race and class issues, including homelessness. Shane (1996) notes that teachers are under-informed about not only the problems faced by homeless students, but also the best strategies they can employ to support them. Teachers themselves report this finding to us over and over again.

Teachers can be a strong and positive force with the right preparation (Duffield et al., 2007), but they have to be made aware of the challenges. There is a strong argument for them being made aware of students' housing situations. Unfortunately, there is no established protocol used by all schools. Some districts keep housing status in the main computer system, where teachers cannot access it; others make the information available if teachers want to look for it; still others use the school social workers as a gatekeeper of students' housing status information (Miller et al., 2015). This can cause frustration for teachers. Robin, a homeless services professional, told us "speaking with teachers, primarily their biggest concern... the biggest takeaway I get from them is that they often have no idea whatsoever if a student is experiencing homelessness." If your school makes it a policy not to share housing information with you, you can nevertheless be on the lookout for signs like those listed in Chapter 2, and you can employ your own methods of finding out (more on this in Chapter 6).

Establishing a safe and caring environment. Once teachers and other school staff have been made aware of the challenges their homeless students face, the focus turns to using that knowledge to create an atmosphere in the school and classroom that communicates security and caring. This is a strategy that is important for the success of all students, but one that stands to benefit unhoused students even more than their peers. The first task in the classroom is to "establish a stable, nonthreatening environment" where students feel welcome (Duffield at al., 2007), a culture that can "provide a respite from the turmoil of uncertainty in the lives of homeless children" (Gewirtzman & Fodor, 1987).

> If a child is tired, I don't press or push...or if they were hungry and they needed some money for a snack or something at the vending machine, I'd give them some money and I don't ask a lot of questions...if you push too hard, then the child becomes embarrassed and then they push away from you as a teacher, and push away from school in general. So I try not to do that. The situation sometimes is bad enough that they don't want to verbalize it...they'll tell you about their situation in their own time.

-Robin, high school teacher

That the school and classroom should be "trustworthy" is echoed in many early recommendations (Eddowes, 1993, p. 384; Gewirtzman & Fodor, 1987). This trustworthy climate, scholars agree, should come in the form of a secure, structured, and predictable atmosphere (Begg et al., 2017) replete with competent and caring adults (Hart-Shegos, 1999). "A sense of 'family' is what these children chiefly need" (Gonzalez, 1990, p. 787), in a place "where opportunities exist for supportive adult relationships" (Ziesemer et al., 1994, p. 667) and students can expect the "discipline as well as love and attention" (Stevens et al., 1991) that may be lacking in their lives because their parents are consumed by survival.

Some authors advocate for the creating of mentoring programs for homeless children (Tierney et al., 2008). Neiman (1988) suggested that these programs can foster students' ability to weather crises by providing them with strong adult role models, and we can see further evidence to support this assertion in recent studies on how positive parenting methods can help children withstand traumatic events such as housing instability (Herbers et al., 2014). While teachers are not parents, it is reasonable to assume that similarly consistent and supportive approaches can provide safety and security for children in the classroom.

Because students without stable housing may have moved around several times in the same school year, teachers should help displaced children feel safe and accepted by encouraging peer connections. "Extraordinary efforts need to be made to foster a sense of membership in the school community" (Ziesemer et al., 1994, p. 666). Eddowes (1993) highlights the active role that sensitive teachers can take in promoting friendships and helping homeless students integrate socially, even though it may be hard for students who move around to forge relationships. They recommend social skill development groups for homeless students: "schools are the child's second most important environment after the family, and the one in which peer relationships are developed" (Ziesemer et al., 1994, p. 667). The Park City elementary school in Dallas, Texas, which has consistently high proficiency scores despite having the most mobile population in the district coupled with the sixth highest poverty rate, uses a buddy system where newly enrolled students are assigned to a friend in the classroom to show them around (Delmore, 2004). Practices such as this can help counteract the social isolation homeless students often experience, as well as orient them to a new situation. Cooperative learning may also help facilitate the social integration of students into the new classroom (Eddowes, 1993). Because we know that homelessness has an impact on an individual's self esteem (Ingram et al., 2016), researchers like Quint (1994) recommend the creation of leadership roles for homeless students, fostering social connections and improving students' sense of empowerment.

Also, recognizing that many homeless students will struggle with mental health challenges like depression and anxiety, as well as problems with withdrawal and aggression, schools should anticipate a need for counseling (Swick, 2000), either by their own school counselors and social workers (Johnson, 1992) or by referral to outside agencies (Delmore, 2004). Provision of appropriate social and emotional support services, including anger management (Delmore, 2004) and mental health service referrals for their parents (Stronge, 1993), can help improve the emotional lives of children experiencing homelessness. Ziesemer and colleagues (1994) have long advocated for teachers to take a role in assisting homeless children and their peers in dealing with loss that comes with high mobility. Kliman (1968) recommended that students be given the chance to express their fears and concerns, because this type of open communication can protect them from stress. Beyond its intrinsic value, improved mental health also increases children's readiness to learn.

Improving learning readiness

When they interviewed unstably housed elementary school children, Horowitz and her team (1988) and Ziesemer and colleagues (1994) found these students enjoyed attending school and took pride in their academic accomplishments. Researchers conclude that schools should take advantage of this positive attitude toward school and channel it into academic success by applying appropriate strategies. "Schools might capitalize on such interest in scholastic competence by communicating high expectations and providing appropriate instruction to achieve those expectations" (Ziesemer et al., 1994, p. 666). Though there is little empirical evidence to support specific academic approaches, there are some themes found in the literature that can guide teachers' actions in the classroom.

Academic program. The most important step in beginning a homeless child's journey to school success is appropriate assessment (Hallett & Skrla, 2017). Many homeless children struggle with the effects of inappropriate educational placement (Stronge, 1993). "Teachers should be skilled in diagnosing and planning for each student's needs," particularly because homeless children's needs can be difficult to diagnose (Eddowes, 1993, p. 384). Some schools have accomplished this via a comprehensive intake interview conducted with students and parents on the first day a student starts at a new school. The intake can include questions designed to elicit from parents whether students received special education support or were involved in special education evaluation at their former school(s) (Delmore, 2004). Johnson (1992) and Duffield and colleagues (2007) recommend an expedited special education evaluation process along with close monitoring by school personnel to ensure that homeless students do not get put at the bottom of waiting lists.

Likewise, the literature suggests that schools should be prepared to provide a continuum of educational options because of the diverse needs of this population, particularly because children experiencing a short episode of homelessness and those who have been without housing for extended periods may have very different needs (Ziesemer et al., 1994), as might the needs of shelter-based children differ from those who are doubled up. Indeed, many parents and students indicate that their time doubled-up was more stressful than other forms of homelessness they experienced (Pavlakis, 2015). Delmore (2004) recommends that schools address the challenge of grade placement by putting children in the correct grade for their ages and then offering extra academic support to bring them up to grade level. Nuñez and Collignon (1997) recommend that students who arrive academically behind be given accelerated, rather than remedial, instruction. However, others recommend focusing on basic skill development (Gonzalez, 1990).

Several researchers recommend special academic support programs for homeless children (Hart-Shegos, 1999; Nuñez & Collignon, 1997). Although the McKinney-Vento Act prohibits schools from segregating homeless children in their own classes, it is nonetheless possible to provide extra services that help enrich their academic skills. "The school must provide a level of support necessary to make learning enjoyable" (Gonzalez, 1990, p. 786). This can take the form of special learning communities or tutoring offered by community volunteers, older students, and/or teachers (Delmore, 2004). Collaborative teacher planning and continuous assessment of student progress can also help accelerate homeless students' learning (Gonzalez, 1990). Close relationships between teachers and students are essential in helping ensure that students' needs do not go unnoticed (Hart-Shegos, 1999).

There is widespread mention in the early literature of using an IEP-style approach where homeless children's academic programs are highly tailored to their individual needs (e.g., Eddowes, 1993; Powers & Jaklitsch, 1993). Gewirtzman and Fodor (1987) noted that highly mobile children tend not to finish tasks, and recommended that instruction be broken down into "small, manageable tasks that children can handle with success" (p. 243). Nuñez and Collignon (1997) describe an instructional process where learning is delivered in short cycles. Ziesemer and colleagues (1994) recommend that schools "offer special instruction to fill academic gaps, communicate high expectations, and provide teaching in small blocks to ensure completion before departure" (p. 667).

> They studied harder, worked harder than a lot of kids because they knew the value of everything we're getting in schools. And they knew without it, they would suffer more.

-Robin, high school teacher

> [They are] street smart, if you will. They have a lot of common sense. They're survivors…. They can fend for themselves…. Surviving. That would be a strength.

-Morgan, 6th grade teacher

Finding strengths. In addition to tailoring learning to individual students' needs, one instructional approach that works well for all students but especially those who are struggling, which is often the case when children are not stably housed, is to identify and build off strengths (Noll & Watkins, 2003). This can be a challenge, because homeless students so frequently come to the classroom with major gaps in their knowledge and skills (recall Jessica from Chapter 2, who was eight years old and did not know the alphabet) but all students do have stores of competence that teachers can find and use to build bridges to academic success. One teacher we spoke to summed up this approach quite nicely:

> It was hard enough for me to make it to school every day growing up, you know, in a suburb with relatively secure financial situations, so if you can make it to school every day with materials ready to roll when you're dealing with those kinds of situations at home, then certainly persistence is a strength that you have. I have a lot of respect for anybody that's gone through it or is going through it. And yeah, I think strength is the operative word there. And persistence because that is such an all-encompassing challenge that affects – I would assume – affects so many arenas of your being. You know, physically, psychologically, so the ability to come and do what you need to do, I think, is pretty special, and is a skill I doubt you lose later on in life. If you've got the scars from that situation then you have the strength from it as well, I'm sure.

-Matthew, 7th grade English teacher

Whether it's homelessness or another major life challenge, our students bring tremendous stores of strength and resilience with them to school every day. Our challenge is to identify the things they do well and can be proud of. Once we have done that, our mindsets change because we believe we are dealing with competent learners who, with proper supports, can accomplish at least as much as their housed peers.

Providing enrichment. The literature on supporting homeless students' education makes frequent mention of providing supportive services before and after school for both tutoring and recreational purposes. Summer programs have been shown to increase homeless students' academic success as well (Sinatra, 2007). In addition to providing students an alternative to spending time on the street or in the shelter (Stevens et al., 1991), before and after school programs can provide crucial academic support, as well as a structured place to complete homework. Because "homeless students have trouble keeping up with work due to the unfavorable study conditions at the shelters" (Gonzalez, 1990, p. 787) or in crowded doubled-up living situations, scholars believe that having an afterschool program where they can simply have space and quiet time to complete assignments is crucial for improving students' performance (Rafferty, 1995).

Tutors in these programs can also help fill in gaps in students' knowledge (Hart-Shegos, 1999). In addition to the potential for direct academic impact, before and after school programs can provide children with meals (Eddowes, 2004), recreational activities (Gewirtzman & Fodor, 1987), and allow them to build bonds with significant adults. "Extracurricular activities...are particularly important for children who have little access to them elsewhere" (Gonzalez, 1990, p. 787; Tierney et al., 2008). Nuñez (1994a) notes the power of extracurricular recreational activities to provide homeless children with self-esteem and social experiences that we know they need (Ingram et al., 2016). Johnson (1992) points out that these programs must be made available free of charge in order for homeless students to be able to participate.

Cross-cutting recommendations

Three additional sets of recommendations from researchers about how schools can support homeless children in school cut across the previous domains of supporting physical and mental health and improving learning readiness: coordinating service delivery and supporting parents. Both of these strategies can be thought to impact multiple facets of unhoused students' lives, potentially supporting their health and mental health and, directly or indirectly, facilitating their learning. We also believe that paying attention to the role of race is an important supportive strategy.

Coordinating services. The literature on supporting homeless people as a group closely parallels the literature on supporting homeless children in school, particularly with regard to the coordination of service delivery (Medcalf, 2008; Tierney et al., 2008). Whether within the school or between schools, shelters, and social service agencies, scholars argue that communication and collaboration are crucial. Indeed, parents in Shields and Warke's (2010) study noted that "one of the major problems was that each person, group, and organization [serving them and their children as they navigate homelessness] seems to work in isolation from all others" (p. 811).

What we were told to do is refer the child to guidance and the school takes care of the rest.

-Robin, high school teacher

I don't know if that system has enough integrity to ensure that that kind of communication is happening. Our counselors are great, but I think, there are like two of them who are like, permanently on staff. It seems like there's other people who come. And that's what I was referring to. There's some people who I don't fully understand their position who I see come on campus occasionally and they're meeting with students. I don't think they have offices here, and I'm not sure exactly what the difference is between what they're doing and our on-site counselors are doing.

-Matthew, 7th grade teacher

As you can see from the teachers quoted above, school approaches to coordination of services for students experiencing homelessness vary dramatically. Researchers have long stressed that communication within the school can assure that all the adults who interact with these high-need students are aware of pressing issues, both ongoing and acute (Gewirtzman & Fodor, 1987). In addition, homeless children need schools to "recognize the interrelationship among their education, social service, health, child welfare, [and] mental health...needs" (Stronge, 1993, p. 356). Julianelle (2007) points out that "a high level of collaboration between professionals" is necessary for homeless student success (p. 39). Though they can take different forms, with services all occurring at school or with students the center of multi-site case management teams (Tierney et al., 2008), the purposes of these collaborative relationships between agencies are similar. They include sharing information so as not to duplicate services (e.g., if students receive tutoring at the shelter, the school does not need to put energy toward finding tutoring for them) and to identify holes in existing services (e.g., if the school nurse notes a potential health issue and can communicate directly with a community health clinic, health care delivery will be more effective). Yon and colleagues (1993) recommend that collaborators establish common goals and work together to meet them. Rouse and Fantuzzo (2009) offer evidence that integrated service systems for all children are more effective then those attempting to work without collaboration, which can be extrapolated to apply to homeless children as well.

Although the effort of reaching out to shelters, service providers, and the community at large may seem burdensome or overstepping of the school's bounds, some believe that no institution is better equipped to serve this crucial role than the school (Newman & Beck, 1996). "Should schools be the main providers of services to homeless students and take on the role of service center? Perhaps not, but they most assuredly must play a fundamental role in developing and implementing integrative services" (Stronge, 1993, p. 357).

Supporting parents. A recommendation commonly found in the literature is that schools should reach out to the parents of homeless children (Swick, 2009). Researchers have found that parents of homeless children are very supportive of and concerned about their children's education (Masten & Sesma, 1999). For several reasons, supporting homeless parents is tantamount to supporting their children, and schools need to focus on making sure parents are included in the education of their children in meaningful ways (Duffield et al., 2007). As we have noted earlier, parents' emotional health impacts their children's emotional health. Supporting parents allows them to be "more emotionally available" for their children (Ziesemer et al., 1994, p. 667).

Researchers recommend that schools involve parents by establishing and maintaining good communication and support them by being knowledgeable about and able to connect parents with medical and social service resources in the community (Myers & Popp, 2003). Masten and colleagues (1997) remind us that teachers and school personnel need to be prepared to build rapport with parents who have no telephones or transportation and "who may be preoccupied with survival needs of their families" (p. 43). Some advise teachers to become advocates in the community for their homeless students' families and to help parents advocate for themselves (Dworsky, 2008).

Although many teacher preparation programs still encourage teachers to get parents involved in their children's schoolwork, recent research casts doubt on whether expecting parents to help children with homework is beneficial; some studies even suggest that parents helping kids with their homework can damage parent-child relationships (Robinson & Harris, 2014). So while we encourage teachers to reach out to unhoused parents and offer support, we are not suggesting that teachers place additional burdens on parents by asking for their direct assistance with their children's academic tasks. In fact, research has demonstrated that the average homeless parent has completed no more than a tenth-grade education and reads at a sixth-grade level (Nuñez, 1994b), so schools would do better to offer parents support (Willard & Kulinna, 2012) and opportunities to further their own education (Swick, 2009) than expect that they help teach their children.

Understanding the role of race

No examination of teaching, especially one focusing on teaching economically disadvantaged children in the United States, can be complete without a consideration of the role of race. Whether we want it to or not, race colors (no pun intended) how we view poverty, schooling, parenting, ideas about community, and ideas about who deserves what. While an in-depth examination of this topic is beyond the scope of this book, we provide a summary of major themes here. (For further development on this topic, *Unconscious Bias in Schools: A Developmental Approach to Exploring Race and Racism* by Sarah Fiarman and Tracey Benson is a fantastic resource, as is *Start Where You Are, But Don't Stay There: Understanding Diversity, Opportunity Gaps, and Teaching in Today's Classrooms* by H. Richard Milner IV).

Children of color, particularly Black and Indigenous/Pacific Islander children, are overrepresented in the homeless population (Ingram et al., 2016). For example, although Black families make up only 14% of American families with children, nearly 50% of sheltered homeless families are Black (Child Trends Data Bank, 2015). People from non-white racial backgrounds are 1.5 times more likely than white people to be homeless, and Black families are three times as likely to be homeless as white families (Bassuk et al., 2014). There is also some overlap between race and help-seeking behavior among unhoused youth; one study found that homeless Black teenagers were less likely than their white homeless peers to self-identify and to take advantage of available services (Ingram et al. 2016). Race is an important factor in the education of children and youth experiencing homelessness.

Representation and mismatch. Over half of the children in public schools in the United States are children of color, while the majority of teachers are white (Fiarman & Benson, 2019). There is no reason a white teacher can't be an effective teacher of children of color – and there are many who are – but research suggests that racial mismatch is likely to harm students of color. Black children who have even one Black teacher in elementary school are 13% more likely to go to college than those who are only ever taught by teachers in whom they cannot see themselves reflected (Gershenson et al., 2018). And students of all races prefer Black teachers (Cherng & Halpin, 2016), but they are in short supply. This imbalance is a challenge to be tackled by teacher preparation programs and pathways, not individual teachers themselves. But teachers, particularly but not exclusively white teachers, need to be aware of the role race plays in how they think about the students in their classrooms. We need to ask ourselves why Black teachers might be more effective for Black children, and whether there's something about that that white teachers can learn from.

This work can be uncomfortable. Research tells us that white teachers punish Black and brown students more often for the same behaviors they let slide from white students (Okonofua & Eberhardt, 2015). We also have to grapple with things like the fact that Black girls are more than twice as likely to be suspended from school as white girls (Love, 2020). While an administrator is ultimately responsible for making the decision to suspend a student, teachers are generally the reason students get referred to the office in the first place. What kinds of expectations or biases lead us to interpret behavior from one group differently than we interpret that same behavior from another group? These are not easy questions.

> I would have them go to a teacher who was Black so that she could relate to them, just to start a conversation, 'cause there was a disconnect because I'm white, it's difficult for the kids to open up to me.

-Erin, high school teacher

Erin's remark here is interesting, and worthy of further examination. On one hand, she evidences understanding that Black students might not feel comfortable coming to her because of their racial mismatch, which demonstrates honesty and introspection on her part. On the other, recognizing that our students don't feel comfortable opening up to us, for whatever reason, is a place to start but not a place to stop (Milner, 2010). Why do her Black students find it difficult to open up to her? What can she do to change this? There is likely something beyond simple skin color match that helps Black students who have Black teachers. Sense of connection, interactional style, high expectations, role modeling, or some constellation of these and other factors may be responsible for the positive correlation researchers have found between Black teachers and school success for Black children. The good news for non-Black teachers is that they too can cultivate connected relationships, hold high expectations for all students, study interactional styles common in different cultural groups, and provide their students with exposure to BIPOC role models. Conversely, Black teachers should not assume that a racial match with their students will be sufficient to facilitate good relationships.

Unconscious bias. Researchers at Harvard have been working on Project

Implicit for over 20 years and have discovered that many of us harbor biases – based on things like race, gender, ethnicity, skin tone, weight – that we might not even know about (Project Implicit, 2021). These biases generally come from sources we don't realize, like the movies and TV we watch, the newspapers, magazines, and websites we read, and the families in which we grew up. But although understanding that we have biases can be uncomfortable, it is crucial work. One reason child homelessness is not well-known in the US may be that it, like poverty in general, disproportionately affects Black families (Ingram et al., 2016). We may not even realize that we are blaming our students' families for their financial situations.

> [T]his idea that…parents, poor parents or Black parents, aren't raising their kids right would be something I would really push back on. If a student is having a struggle, everyone should pitch in and accept responsibility for that. Looking at the real societal issues that position students to fail…that disproportionately affect, like Black, brown, and poor students…realizing how those issues affect the students that are in my room, and then looking at people who are privileged to be in the middle class position of teaching as opposed to the students that are in the room, and the cultural conflicts that can arise, the cultural misunderstandings that can arise when you haven't really examined those things or examined your own presuppositions.

-Matthew, 7th grade English

Matthew makes good points, and we will see more in Chapter 6 about how surrounding ourselves with like-minded colleagues can prevent us from falling to the trap of scapegoating homeless, low-SES, and/or non-white students and parents for things that are really the results of systems in our society.

It is particularly problematic that we see racism, possibly unconscious, in school outcomes like discipline (Hope et al., 2014). Put simply, students of color are much more likely than white students to be suspended or expelled from school. When those students are also from low-SES backgrounds or facing additional challenges like homelessness, outcomes get even worse. As we will learn more about in Chapter 5, students who have suffered or are suffering traumas in their lives often act out in ways that we have been conditioned to see as defiant or purposefully disruptive, and we've been trained to punish them accordingly. But student resistance to teacher directives can teach us a lot about where our practice needs to improve (Toshalis, 2015), whether that means the school or classroom feels unsafe to students of color, homeless students, students of a certain gender, or a myriad diversity of student identities and realities. None of us wants to believe we contribute to a culture of racial inequality in our schools and classrooms, but many of us nonetheless do. The good news is that by increasing our awareness, we can change this.

Conclusions

Homeless children are faced with many issues that have the potential to interfere with their educational success. Some of these challenges are also present in the lives of housed poor children, though homeless children often experience problems at greater rates or in more depth than their housed peers. The school has several important roles to play in supporting these students, falling into the realms of eliminating legal and procedural barriers in accordance with McKinney-Vento legislation, supporting students' physical needs, facilitating their mental health, and increasing educational readiness. In addition, there is an additional category of recommendations around coordinating services within and among schools and other service providers, supporting parents, and being honest about the role of race and racism in teaching undomiciled students when most teachers are white but most students are not. Some researchers and advocates believe that schools have an imperative to provide services to homeless students, one of the most vulnerable groups we serve in education. "Schools *must* take the lead in making the difference for these children" (Medcalf, 2008, p. 109, emphasis added).

Chapter 4

How can we help students who are graduating?

Several factors contribute to homelessness among adolescents. "Youth most often cite family conflict as the major reason for their homelessness...a youth's low-income family dynamics, sexual activity, sexual orientation, pregnancy, school problems, and alcohol and drug use are strong predictors of family discord" that may lead a youth to leave or be told to leave home (Fernandes-Alcantara, 2019, p. 5). As we will discuss in more detail in Chapter 5, these problems often follow students into the classroom. Unstable living environments and family conflict harm students' academic success. "The experience of homelessness itself can be highly destabilizing, even traumatic, with effects on a student's physical, mental, financial, and academic well-being" (NCHE, 2015, p. 2). Homelessness affects students' lives in ways that they cannot always control, but we know that a college degree will help students overcome their circumstances. We need to use a holistic approach to encourage and support these students in their transition to college.

Best practices for preparing undomiciled students for college

Students have many different reasons for wanting to go to college. Some may wish to further their education, prepare for a career, or get away from their parents and have a fun social experience at college. For some, a degree opens doors to many new opportunities and creates a different way of life. Earning a college degree is not an easy task, nor is getting into college. Some students and schools start preparing for college as early as the eighth grade. But what about students whose parents can't help them prepare or aren't in their lives at all? Before students take their first college class, hundreds of questions go through their minds. The Free Application for Federal Student Aid (FAFSA) has 108 questions (Federal Student Aid, 2019). What are some of the questions undomiciled students have about college?

The college process is challenging to navigate, and even with support from parents, teachers, and friends, it can still be a tense time. Students who start the college choice process have many things to consider. Adding the additional stress of having unstable housing can affect a student's college decision-making, or even whether they apply to college at all. College choice is a process with three stages: 1) predisposition, 2) search, and 3) choice (Perna, 2006). Predisposition refers to the mindset of a student who has already decided to apply to college. Higher levels of self-efficacy may positively impact students experiencing homelessness (Havlik et al., 2018). Their grit and determination to attend college, given their adverse situation, should be commended and supported. The college aspirations of students who experience homelessness are grounded in a desire for upward mobility, a chance to escape their living conditions. Perhaps because they have seen how their parents' low educational attainment creates hardships for them (Nuñez, 1994b), students who have experienced homelessness seem to value educational success more than their housed peers (Begg et al., 2017).

The second stage, search, refers to the period of time when students submit college applications, write essays, take the SAT or ACT, send their score reports to schools, and provide FAFSA information. This second stage requires more commitment than predisposition, which is simply a desire to attend. It requires several actions on the student's behalf. Even the Common Application, which allows students to apply to multiple colleges at once, still evaluates their level of commitment and desire to attend college. The third stage is choice, when students narrow down the search and decide which college they will attend. Although we often see pictures on social media or news articles where a deserving student has offers and millions of dollars in scholarships from multiple colleges and universities, these experiences are not the norm and even these lucky students can only attend one college at a time. The choice school is the one college students will enroll in and hopefully graduate from.

Preparing for college

What are some things teachers can do in the classroom to assist undomiciled students in preparing for college? Helping students to become aware of the possibility of attending college is essential, and can begin even before high school. Building students' college knowledge is critical. What is college knowledge? Friedman (2019) states, "college knowledge includes an understanding of the options that exist beyond high school" (p.1). Many of our undomiciled students may not be able to see past the challenges of surviving their day-to-day situations. College can provide a goal on which they can focus, almost an escape from their troubles. College knowledge also includes familiarity with college jargon and language. Do students know what a dorm is, what room and board means, the meanings of titles like "Dean" and "Professor," processes like admission, housing lottery, meal plan choice? Do they know that college students pick a major, generally have some control over what classes they take and when? Do they know how many hours a week most college students are in class?

College is an extension of K-12 education in some ways, but in other, fundamental, ways, it is quite different. A student who is overburdened by five 7-hour high school days in a week may assume that a college schedule would be equally intolerable and shy away. Given the knowledge that most college students spend only 12-15 hours per week in class and have the opportunity to select courses that interest them at times that fit their schedules, many more students might consider college a viable option. Ardoin (2018) found that college knowledge was an additional obstacle for rural students from poor and working-class backgrounds, especially those who were first-generation students. Because college completion is lower for low-SES groups, college knowledge is likely to be an obstacle for our students experiencing homelessness as well.

Another piece of college jargon is "FAFSA." Many students are told to fill it out, but do they know how to fill it out? Moreover, they need fill it out correctly and completely, but how can students without parental support complete all the questions? To complete the FAFSA, all 108 questions must be answered and additional documents must be submitted. We will go further into the details of the FAFSA process related to students experiencing homelessness later in this chapter, but for now, let us stick to the basics of what the FAFSA is: the Free Application for Federal Student Aid. As a FAFSA coach, Brandy has seen students pay companies to complete a free application! It is in the name, it is free. Students should never pay to complete a FAFSA form, but they may not know that they can do it themselves.

Underdeveloped college knowledge can cause students to waste time and money. This is an area where teachers can help develop students' understanding by explaining terms fully or providing additional information that describes the material details. Other words terms that might be unfamiliar to students include: placement test, best fit, application term, and type of admission. Websites like First in the Family (www.firstinthefamily.org) include more information that can be helpful to students with low college knowledge. This information is also available in multiple languages, which can help English learners understand and feel comfortable with the subject matter.

FAFSA is a comprehensive application that colleges use to determine students' eligibility for student aid and determine their financial aid packages. It includes grants, federal loans, and some scholarships. Some states also use FAFSA information to determine whether students qualify for state aid. The FAFSA application is the only place in the college process that asks whether a student is homeless, but it is not a simple yes or no question. In most cases, students who indicate that they unhoused are then required to provide documentation called a homelessness determination. Determining if a student is unaccompanied can be done by the school or district, a homeless shelter director funded by the United States Department of Housing and Urban Development, or a youth runaway or homeless center director (Federal Student Aid, 2021). If students indicate here that they are unaccompanied, they will not be asked to provide their parents' financial information. They still do, however, need to provide a mailing address where financial aid award paperwork can be sent. This obviously presents a challenge for undomiciled youth, who may not be able to predict where they will be staying. Teachers can offer the school's address or even their own, if they are comfortable with this, so students can receive mail.

In most cases, if a student indicates that they are homeless and can provide documentation, their award package is processed a little faster. Most students experiencing homelessness will have a zero Estimated Family Contribution, which may result in a refund. Students can then use the refund for housing-related expenses. For most undomiciled students, the FAFSA is the only way of making college affordable and having stable housing. Unfortunately, even free room and board award is not a guarantee of year-round housing. Some colleges close their dorms during breaks or charge students to stay in them over the summer. And when Covid forced the closing of residential housing last year to slow the spread of the virus, some students had nowhere to return (Stauffer, 2021).

To complete the FAFSA, students must also have tax information from one or two of the previous tax sessions and a parent's signature. Tax documents are a significant barrier for students who have family conflicts, run away from home, or have no contact with their biological parents, unless they can get documentation of unaccompanied status. Each institution's financial aid office can make an exception for extenuating circumstances, however. Teachers can assist unhoused students in the process by first telling them to apply as soon as possible. The FAFSA opens on October 1 every year. Some financial aid is doled out on a first-come, first-served basis, so it is in their best interest to apply early. The Higher Education Opportunity Act of 2008 also expanded access to programs that can help students connect with colleges and make the transition free of charge. Advanced Placement, SAT, and ACT exam fees can also usually be waived (Hallett & Skrla, 2017). Teachers should encourage students to get in touch with guidance counselors who know about the processes of applying for such waivers.

Second, teachers can help by informing students to get in touch with the financial aid office at their school of choice as soon as possible. Teachers may need to advocate for them as well. One outstanding example of this can be seen in the documentary The Homestretch, where we see a student's teacher not only take him in to her house but guide him through the college application process and even go with him to meet with officials at his school of choice. Obviously, not every teacher can (or should) go above and beyond like this for every student, but their journey is an inspirational one and may spark ideas about how we can better connect our unhoused students with colleges. Reaching out to the school of choice is important because each institution's process is slightly different; knowing the process specific to that school can save the student a lot of time and frustration.

Another critical point about the FAFSA is that it is an annual application, meaning students will have to apply again on their own after they've graduated. Completing the application for our students will not build in them the capacity to do it themselves the next year. A student experiencing homelessness will have to go through this challenging process every year until they become independent. Independent status is usually reached when a student is 24 years of age, has a child or is married (Federal Student Aid, 2020). Unfortunately, Brandy has known students who waited until they were 24 years old because it was just too difficult for them to do when the system considered them dependents, and they did not know who to reach out to for help.

College access and success for a student experiencing homelessness is an under-researched topic that is starting to grow. The Hope Center for College, Community, and Justice leads the most significant studies on basic needs and insecurities. In 2019, nearly 167,000 students from 171 two-year institutions and 56 four-year institutions took part in a national survey called #RealCollege (Hope Center for College, Community, and Justice (Hope Center), 2019). They found that 39% of respondents had been food insecure in the preceding 30 days, 46% of respondents were housing insecure in the previous year, and 17% of respondents had experienced homelessness in the year before the survey (Goldrick-Rab et al.,

2019). The most recent survey, conducted during the pandemic, found that nearly three of out five students experienced basic needs insecurities (Hope Center, 2021). As more research focuses on basic needs, schools and universities are becoming aware of these issues and creating programs and services that support students.

Some unique solutions to addressing students' basic needs have been gaining popularity. Principal Abkar Cook of West Side High School in Newark, New Jersey, installed a free laundromat because an undomiciled student was being bullied for having dirty clothes (Dawson, 2018). Another program is the Tacoma Housing Authority, which provides rental assistance for Tacoma Community College students who are enrolled and are experiencing homelessness (Tacoma Community College, 2021). This is a prime example of an outside agency working together with a college to support unhoused students. SchoolHouse Connection also has a library of resources and webinars on its website, as well as scholarships that teachers can tell students about.

Conclusions

Hidden homelessness is what we mostly see in education, which makes it difficult to assist and address the needs of undomiciled students as they prepare for college. Creating a college-going culture with college knowledge for all students, especially addressing the barriers of unhoused students, is vital. In the classroom, teachers can play a significant role by increasing their own awareness of the challenges students face and connecting students with supports as they begin to plan for their lives post-graduation. Undomiciled students are often in a constant stage of transition due to their lack of stable housing. The additional transition from high school to college may feel too overwhelming to navigate alone, and some students disregard college altogether. With the support of teachers, the transition does not have to be debilitating, and teachers can be the support they need.

Chapter 5

What is the role of trauma in homeless students' lives?

When the flood happened, when the water was coming, they grabbed their school uniforms and everything, and their school supplies…but everything else they left behind.

-Robin, high school teacher

Much attention has been paid recently in educational research and literature about trauma: what it is, where it comes from, and how it affects children's lives, particularly their learning and their classroom behavior. While not all children who experience trauma will become homeless and not all homeless children have been traumatized, there is a strong correlation between the two experiences. Harsh experiences of stress, trauma, and loss are all too familiar to many undomiciled children (Wade et al., 2014). In fact, for many children, the very experience of losing shelter itself can constitute a traumatic experience: losing their homes, their belongings, their connections to neighborhood and friends, having to surrender beloved pets, often having to split from some family members, sometimes changing schools. Trauma has been "found to be both a cause and a consequence of homelessness" (Collins, 2013, p. 61). Reasons for the loss of housing are also often rooted in trauma, such as an escape from domestic violence or natural disaster displacement. In this chapter, we examine trauma, sometimes referred to as traumatic stress, as well as stress and chronic stress, and the impacts each can have on students' social, emotional, academic, and even physical health. We will also look at classroom approaches believed to provide support for children who have experienced trauma.

Stress

We have all experienced stress in our lives: an important job interview, a difficult test in school, a big sporting event. While events like these can be unpleasant to endure, and exposure to too many of them can have effects on our emotional health, these commonplace, short-duration stressful experiences are not what researchers mean when they talk about traumatic or chronic stress. Particularly as it relates to children, research on traumatic or chronic stress refers to experiences that activate our defenses over and over again to the extent that our bodies cannot recover properly. Let's use the difficult test example. You've most likely taken a test in your life for which you felt un-prepared. You might have had worried thoughts before and during the test, and experienced physical symptoms like a racing pulse, shaky hands, and sweating. For a detailed explanation of the science behind exactly what happens, involving the hypothalamic-pituitary-adrenal axis and the amygdala, you can check out Dr. Nadine Burke-Harris's book *The Deepest Well: Healing the Long-Term Effects of Childhood Adversity* (2018) or her TED talk, but you probably know this phenomenon by a common name instead, your fight-or-flight response. Perhaps you've heard about adrenaline, the chemical released when we perceive danger (whether that danger is physical or the threat of failing trigonometry), or cortisol, another hormone related to the body's stress response. What's important to know is that when we experience stressful events, our bodies produce a physical response that ends when the stressful event ends. It's also important to know that while the stress response isn't harmful in these kinds of situations, and can even be helpful (particularly if we're in some sort of physical danger), it is nonetheless exhausting for our bodies. They need time to recover. We were not meant to live in a constant state of fight or flight.

Chronic stress

As the name implies, chronic stress is stress that either doesn't end, or re-occurs so frequently that our bodies do not have time to recover between episodes. Imagine if you had a test as stressful as the hypothetical one we just discussed every week or even every day. Eventually, your body's ability to fight or flee would change. You might become exhausted and start to experience things like irritability, headaches, and trouble sleeping. Or your response might get stuck in the "on" position, meaning you'd be on high alert constantly, anxious and perceiving threats where none actually existed, because your brain had become so conditioned to expect danger. With chronic stress, the body's response does not end when the stressful event ends (or the event never truly ends), which might have dangerous consequences for adults. For children, the effects can be catastrophic.

Trauma

More severe than stress, "trauma occurs when a child experiences an intense event that threatens or causes harm to his or her emotional and physical well-being" (National Child Traumatic Stress Network, 2003, p. 1). Also called traumatic stress, trauma is similar to chronic stress in that it causes a problem in the body's fight-or-flight response system. A shocking, life-changing event like escaping a flooding home during a storm, or surviving a violent assault, can trigger a fight-or-flight response that never properly shuts off. Continuing the trigonometry test example from the last section, trauma would be as if the building burned down while you were taking the test. Akin to post-traumatic stress disorder (PTSD), trauma triggers responses in our bodies that can leave people constantly re-living a terrible event. While the trauma we speak of here is not exactly the same as PTSD, it can sometime cause similar symptoms. Both involve the person experiencing long-lasting emotional and physical distress even after the event is over. "Past experiences can live on in the body and may be experienced as flashbacks, memories, or repetitive thoughts about the painful event" (Desautels, 2016).

Adverse Childhood Experiences (ACEs)

Traumatic experiences, recent medical research has discovered, can actually rewire the brain, particularly when they occur during childhood. Leading medical researchers Felitti and Anda (1998) asked over 15,000 adults about traumatic experiences they'd had as children, and then determined which ones were causally linked to adult mental and physical health problems. Known as Adverse Childhood Experiences or ACEs, the ten childhood experiences now believed to cause actual physical changes to the brain and body are: physical, emotional, or sexual abuse; physical or emotional neglect; parent with a mental health or substance dependence problem; witnessing domestic violence; having an incarcerated parent; and parents' divorce (CDC, 2019). These childhood events have been connected to adult physical outcomes like cancer, heart disease, substance dependence, and premature death. They can also be connected to mental health outcomes later in life, like suicidality, depression, and anxiety. But even before children become adults, their ACEs impact their lives. It's important to think about what really happens when a trauma affects a child, but also how common these experiences are for homeless children. Researchers have found that 67% of adults in the US experience at least one ACE, and almost 13% had four or more (Burke-Harris, 2018). We know that homeless students are likely to have experienced more than the general population.

Abuse is a common ACE, whether it is physical, emotional, sexual, or aimed at someone else in the household. And we also know that a higher-than-average number of homeless children have spent time in foster care because of abuse. Although both low-SES housed and homeless children are likely to have been exposed to family violence, the homeless children in Buckner and colleagues' (1999) study had significantly higher rates of lifetime sexual abuse (Johnson et al., 2006) and foster care involvement, leading researchers to conclude that homeless children had greater exposure to traumatic events, which we now term ACEs, than their housed low-SES counterparts. Unsurprisingly, children placed in foster care have higher ACE scores on average than the general population (Turney & Wildeman, 2017). There is crossover between homelessness and foster care. Alperstein and colleagues (1988) found that homeless children suffered higher rates of abuse than housed low-SES children, and more recent studies confirm this finding (e.g., Anooshian, 2005; Gewirtz & Edleson, 2007). We know that in at least one study, children experiencing homelessness were 34 times more likely to have spent time in foster care than children overall (Institute for Children, Poverty, & Homelessness, 2017).

We can't know for sure that rates of abuse are actually higher for this population. It's possible that homeless children are simply more likely to have social workers examining their lives than are housed children. Nevertheless, we can be sensitive to the possibility that students experiencing homelessness may have suffered traumatic experiences like abuse or neglect. If the home situation was severe enough to lead to children being removed from their parents, they are more likely to have been exposed to ACEs like parental divorce, parental death, and parental mental health/substance use disorders than other children (Turney & Wildeman, 2017). And when children are removed from the home, that removal itself constitutes a trauma. Even if their parents are abusive, "study after study demonstrates that children also suffer complex and long-lasting harms when they are removed from their parents and placed into foster care" (Trivedi, 2019, p. 593). This is not only because additional abuse often happens in foster homes (New Jersey Office of the Child Advocate, 2008) but because the bonds between children and parents are strong, even when those parents are unable to provide stable care.

Other nations are much more focused on family preservation than we are in the United States. Scandinavian countries in particular put many more resources toward supporting parents to the point where it is safe for their children to remain with them, rather than compounding kids' trauma with separation and placement in the hands of strangers (Khoo et al., 2002). Included in supports that might be offered to a family in crisis are "adequate housing, decent day care, medical and dental services for the children, and economically viable parent leave from the workforce" and "whenever things do go wrong, the government's policy is to de-stigmatize social services" (p. 467). As a result, children in countries like these spend less time in out-of-home placements and parents are much less likely to have their children removed from them permanently.

But here in the US, children who suffer abuse and neglect at home are much more likely to end up with the further trauma of being taken away from the caregivers they've bonded with since birth. We often overlook this trauma, thinking instead that the best placement for any child is away from parents who abuse or neglect them. And while we obviously all want children to be safe, we need to reframe our thinking and understand that any child who has been removed from their family home is likely suffering immensely. Foster care is not necessarily better, and in many cases it is worse, than what was happening in the biological family. We may see behaviors in school that reflect what children are going or have been through. And life after foster care may not be better: one study in Texas found that 50% of teens exited foster care into homelessness, and 70% had at least one mental health disorder (White et al., 2012).

Housing and chronic stress/trauma

To recap, *stress* is an event that activates our fight-or-flight response, but the event ends and our bodies have time to recover. *Chronic stress*, sometimes called *toxic stress*, is when stressful events never end, or keep recurring so often that our bodies cannot recover in between episodes. Likewise, *trauma* is an acute event so upsetting to a person that they continue to experience physical and emotional responses even after the event has ended and the danger has passed. Chronic stress and trauma, while not good for anyone, can have especially negative and long-lasting effects on the brains and bodies of children. A fight-or-flight response that never shuts off can cause long-term physical effects. Brain structure changes and even changes to our DNA (Burke-Harris, 2018) can occur as a result of too much chronic/toxic stress or trauma during childhood. Research suggests that children who experience homelessness are more likely to have had trauma in their lives than children in stable housing, especially because the loss of housing can be traumatic in itself. We can't know everything about students from their housing statuses, but the information can give us reason to suspect houseless children have been through a lot.

Trauma and learning

Children experiencing homelessness are more likely than their housed low-SES peers to have certain types of traumatic stress in their lives (Grant et al., 2007a). One common trauma may occur when family members are forced to separate in order to get housing. Many shelters only accept women and young children (Duffield & Lovell, 2008). The United States Conference of Mayors (1991) reported that 62% of families surveyed had had to break up before entering the shelter system. Some parents choose to place their children with relatives or friends before seeking temporary shelter to spare them the experience (Mihaly, 1991). If relatives or friends are not able to offer housing, children whose parents lose their housing may be placed in foster care (National Black Child Development Association, 1989), where they are likely to have negative experiences (Trivedi, 2019). Likewise, homeless children are more likely to have been separated from their families and involved in the foster care system at some point in their lives even before their episode of homelessness (Hart-Shegos, 1999).

On top of the extreme familial stressors homeless children are likely to suffer, the very experience of homelessness itself adds the stress of disruption and loss (Rafferty & Shinn, 1991). Losing one's home means losing treasured possessions; relocating means severing social ties and routines (Mihaly, 1991), all of which extract an emotional toll. Schmitz et al. (1995) state, "moving creates a situational crisis which can result in increased stress, anxiety, anger, sadness, and a lowered sense of competence" (p. 313). Children in homeless families may also be forced early into adult roles of helping to care for younger children, to find food, and to secure lodging, and this disruption of child and parental roles can cause stress and tension within the family (Mihaly, 1991). Two thirds of homeless children worry about having enough to eat (NCFH, 2009), a distinctly stressful and very adult concern.

Moreover, shelters themselves can present emotionally taxing living conditions. Crowded and noisy congregate living quarters cause stress for parents and children. Though many cities have improved their shelter systems for homeless families, congregate shelters still exist in some places. "Most mothers are acutely stressed while living in a shelter and their scores on measures of psychological distress are comparable to those of psychiatric outpatients" (Buckner et al., 1999, p. 246). Mihaly (1991) explains that there is an "unquantifiable loss of family cohesion and parental authority when meals are no longer prepared and eaten together" (p. 5), as is often the case in temporary shelters. Boxhill and Beaty (1990) interviewed homeless mothers in Atlanta and reported that many were upset by having their roles as the primary nurturer, provider, and decision-maker for their families taken over by shelter policies, procedures, and personnel, leading them to lose confidence in their parenting abilities. Gewirtzman and Fodor (1987) remind us that maternal stress leads to decreased time and attention to devote to parenting, increasing children's stress. Lupien and team (2005) found a significant correlation between maternal depression and children's stress level. Rubin and colleagues (1996) found that a mother's depression and length of homeless episode appear to be underlying mechanisms influencing her children's test scores. Although not all children without homes will experience trauma, when we learn that students are experiencing homelessness, we need to be aware of everything else that might be going on in their lives.

Beyond the relatively clear connection between stress and mental health problems, research shows that children who experience a great deal of stress may also have profound difficulties learning (Bassuk et al., 2014). It has been well-known for decades that children from low-SES backgrounds have elevated exposure to acute and chronic stressors (McLoyd, 1998), but until recently no causal mechanism had been discovered between stress and academic functioning. However, in 2009, Evans and Schamberg combined studies of neurocognition and physiological stress and postulated a link between SES, stress, and memory function in children that might help explain the income-test score gap and shed light on the problems homeless children experience in school. Their groundbreaking study demonstrated that children from low-SES backgrounds in the sample had significantly higher allostatic loads (a physical measure of the body's chemical response to stress) than children from high-SES backgrounds, and that allostatic load was correlated with working memory. The highly-stressed children from low-SES backgrounds in the study could hold significantly fewer items in their working memory than those from high-SES homes (Evans & Schamberg, 2009). If, as this research suggests, the increased stress of growing up in poverty leads to chemical changes in the brain that affect working memory, low-SES children may literally have a harder time learning. This complements earlier work by Noble, McCandliss, and Farah (2007), wherein SES was found to be a significant predictor of working memory in first graders.

Lupien and team (2005) also found that the low-SES children in their study had higher levels of cortisol (the so-called "stress hormone") and manifested differences in cognitive function. Earlier studies established that children growing up with environmental stress (e.g., noise) had higher blood pressure and less capacity to discriminate between relevant and irrelevant tasks, a measure of the selective attention that is crucial to learning (Cohen et al., 1973). It is possible that growing up in poverty causes children to be less able to learn than their less-stressed high-SES peers. This could also help explain why homeless children in some cases have worse school performance than their housed low-SES peers, as some studies have identified that homeless children are likely to have been exposed more recently to major stressors like moving or abuse (Buckner et al., 1999). "Even among very poor families, homelessness appears to be associated with lower income and more recent adversity" (Masten et al., 1993, p. 341).

She was living with her father at the time, then he choked her, so her friends decided that she had to get out. [The] guidance counselors, they gave her a list of all the services she qualified for, and they were able to find her a place to live. They had to transfer schools…but the main thing was she had to get out of her dad's house.

-*Robin, high school teacher*

Exposure to trauma is high among both homeless children and their parents (Anooshian, 2005). One study of homeless families in three types of housing programs found that 93% of mothers had experienced at least one trauma and 81% experienced multiple traumatic events. 79 % experienced trauma in childhood, 82% in adulthood, and 91% in both adulthood and childhood. Violent victimization was the most common traumatic experience: 70% reported being physically assaulted by a family member or someone they knew and approximately half had been sexually assaulted (Hayes et al., 2013).

How trauma manifests in the classroom

Knowing what we do about the impacts of trauma on the developing brain, it does not come as a surprise that children who have high ACE scores tend to struggle in school. Both behavior and academics are impacted by trauma, and unless schools and classrooms change to be supportive and responsive to this, it's not hard to imagine that high rates of dropout will continue to plague the homeless student population.

Lashing out

As we've noted previously in this volume, homeless children's stress and trauma can manifest in seemingly contradictory ways: some children internalize, meaning they may become withdrawn or depressed, while other externalize, meaning they may have angry outbursts that seem out of proportion to those around them.

> If something was to trigger them, they outlash. Fearing you're coming for them and violating their space, they'll lash out with anger, just for no reason. If you say something, rub them the wrong way, they just lash out.

-Stephen, 8th grade teacher

Although Stephen's characterization above likely reflects a generalization he reached based on a limited sample of homeless students, it is likely that the behaviors he describes above are connected to trauma in students' lives. One common manifestation of trauma in the classroom is what's called *hypervigilance*, a state in which the fight-or-flight response is always on (Lacoe, 2013), so students have a hard time distinguishing between minor annoyances and actual threats to their safety. These are kids who seem ready to fight over the smallest issue, kids who flip a desk when someone accidentally bumps into them walking by. They may also lash out verbally in ways that seem disproportionate to the situation, in response to small slights or even no slights that the teacher can detect. Unfortunately, many teachers have been conditioned, or even explicitly trained, to interpret such behavior as "defiance" or "disrespect," particularly when it comes from Black students (Gregory & Weinstein, 2008) rather than to read in it clear signs that a child is feeling unsafe. And when teachers or schools respond to such behavior with harsh punishments, this usually exacerbates the problem.

> She was very angry...like, really sweet kid [but] one of those turn-on-a-dime kind of personalities, where she would just come in...very eager to please, even in simple

ways, you know, "can I write it like this or that?" But then at certain times that sort of oppositional anger about small things would surface too. [She] was expelled by the end of the year. And then another kid came in a few days later…[he] only lasted I think two days here. He came in, just very angry and aggressive and just completely seemed out of touch with like the classroom environment in general…just really out of step and flew off the handle at a kid almost immediately after being placed in the room.

-Matthew, 7th grade teacher

If we imagine that the children Matthew describes above come from safe, loving households with plumbing, heat, electricity, and enough food to eat, it can be easy to assume that they are simply misbehaving, just kids in need of strict punishments to curb their behavior, or even kids who are just not compatible with school. But if we take a moment to imagine that both of the students he describes have experienced or are experiencing ACEs, we can see that the behaviors he saw might be manifestations of trauma. Given that experts believe two thirds of public school children will experience at least one traumatic event in their lives (CDC, 2019), it is reasonable to try to view problematic behavior through this lens, especially when it comes from children with unstable housing. We become better teachers of undomiciled students when we remember that lack of housing so often comes with a constellation of other risk factors for trauma and ACEs.

One of the most interesting findings of recent years in brain research is that our "fight-or-flight" response system actually has two other options, dubbed "freeze" and "fawn" (Walker, 2013). The first is self-explanatory – sometimes we freeze up in a stressful or dangerous situation. This can have protective effects if a predator can be evaded by simply freezing and remaining undetected. Whether that predator is a T. rex or an abusive parent, the response makes sense. The "fawn" response refers to an autonomic reaction to danger that tells our bodies to try to placate whoever is endangering us, to try to please them, to make them happy so they don't try to hurt us. We can see echoes of the "fawn" response in the young lady Matthew describes, who seems overly eager to please the teacher, perhaps because being overly accommodating, or "fawning," over an abuser at home keeps her out of harm's way. But she also evidences a tendency to overreact to small things, which might be when her system tells her that "fight" is the best way to be safe. In either case, her body's response system is probably not operating optimally. The behaviors that got her kicked out of school were very likely a response to dangers her body perceived because of things that happened outside of school. Likewise, the boy he describes is almost a textbook example of hypervigilance, possibly because in other environments, he has to be on alert all the time in order to stay physically or emotionally safe. We can be relatively sure that in neither case did expelling the students from school serve their best interests.

Internalizing

Just as previous research indicated that students experiencing homelessness might exhibit the emotional strain by either externalizing behaviors like aggression or by internalizing ones like shyness, withdrawal, and anxiety, so too can trauma take either form. So while students who externalize as a result of their traumatic experiences tend to get the most attention from teachers, for the obvious reason that they disrupt the classroom and everyone else's learning, we also need to keep an eye on students who are overly withdrawn or who seem excessively nervous, depressed, or anxious. These, too, can be manifestations of trauma.

Trauma-responsive approaches

There is research to support the use of trauma-informed work with homeless mothers (Hayes et al., 2013). SchoolHouse Connection, a national non-profit dedicated to overcoming homelessness through education, recommends that we extrapolate and assume such approaches will also be beneficial to their children, or even to young people who are homeless without their families (2012). The first thing we can do as teachers is to shift how we think about problem behaviors in the classroom. When a child acts out, or seems excessively quiet, instead of asking "what's wrong with you?" if we can move ourselves to asking "what happened to you?" we can make a crucial change. Recognizing that even the most difficult behaviors come from some experience a child has had or is having, we can start to look for solutions. A traumatized child is not trying to push your buttons or get a rise out of you; in reality, most children are not trying to make teachers angry. Resources abound to help you dig deeper into this topic, from *Educational Leadership's* 2019 issue on safe schools to Kristin Souers & Pete Hall's *Fostering Resilient Learners: Strategies for Creating a Trauma-Sensitive Classroom* (2016) and Karen Gross's *Trauma Doesn't Stop at the School Door: Strategies and Solutions for Educators, PreK-College* (2020).

Obviously, as teachers, we are mandated reporters, so if we have children whose behavior leads us to suspects abuse or neglect at home, especially if we have any other evidence to corroborate our suspicions, we are required to tell someone. Who we are required to tell depends on the state in which we teach. If this information hasn't been provided to you already, it is usually easy to find on the internet. But knowing what we do about the trauma that removal and foster care can cause, we want to make very sure we have reliable reason to suspect a child is in danger. Unfortunately, race plays a role here as well; Black children are more likely to be removed from their families and have longer stays in foster care than white children (Dettlaff, 2015). These racial disparities are seen at every stage of the process: Black children are more likely to be reported for suspected abuse and more likely to be removed because of such a report. Doctors may be influenced by implicit racial bias, since they refer Black children to child protective services more often than white children, even when the Black children's injuries are less severe (Diyaolu et al., 2021).

The report is only one step. Next, we have to find ways to de-escalate situations where students are out of control or having outsized reactions to classroom stimuli. It's likely the cause of the behavior has already ended, but we are still left to deal with the aftermath in the classroom. The first step to responding appropriately to student trauma is to expect it. Research clearly links trauma with difficulty self-regulating, uncontrolled negative thinking, hypervigilance (being on high alert for danger), difficulty trusting adults, and inappropriate social interactions (Lacoe,

2013; Terrasi & de Galarce, 2017), so when we see these behaviors, we should assume that there is a traumatic explanation. The next step is to help students feel safe. This area of research is still somewhat new and evolving, but experts generally agree on a few broad categories of support for trauma-based learners, which can be applied to those with housing as well.

Forge relationships through thoughtful interactions

Making sure we speak to students in ways that work for them can help create a feeling of safety. Safety is first and foremost about controlling one's environment. Traumatized children have likely experienced frightening situations over which they had no control. Consider ways to give students choices rather than issuing mandates. Sharing your classroom control with difficult students can feel counterintuitive, but Minahan and Rappaport (2012) give the example of a teacher who asked a hard-to-reach student questions like "would you like to stand in the front of the line or the back of the line?" instead of telling him "line up!" The former worked well for the student, while the latter was likely to end in an explosive event that exhausted both him and his teacher. Likewise, some students respond much better to private behavior redirections, such as a sticky note subtly placed on a student's desk asking her to turn her attention back to her work, rather than a verbal "be quiet" within earshot of her peers. Toshalis (2015) reminds us that there is always a reason for student misbehavior (which he labels "resistance," a thought-provoking reframing) in the classroom. It is our job to figure out that reason and see whether we can minimize students' feelings that they are unsafe in our classrooms.

Predictability is safety

Most children (and adults) feel safer in predictable environments. We like to know what is coming next. This can be especially true of children with ADHD (Manna, 2009) and students who have experienced trauma. Something as simple as posting a daily schedule on the board – and sticking to it – can help traumatized students know what to expect, enhancing a feeling that school is predictable and therefore safe. Begg and her colleagues (2017) found that houseless third through sixth graders specifically identified predictability as a tool they used to envision a safe future for themselves. Interestingly, this is a courtesy that we already extend to adult learners. When you attend a conference or professional development session, for example, you expect to be given an agenda of what will happen at what times and you may even feel irritated or anxious if the presenter does not adhere to the schedule. Likewise, posting reasonable classroom rules and the logical consequences for violating them, and then calmly and consistently enforcing the consequences, creates a feeling of predictability and safety that benefits all students but can be a game-changer for traumatized children.

It is important to remember that students, regardless of their age, trauma history, or housing status, are never going to tell you that rules and consequences make them feel safe. They probably don't even know it's true. And the closer they get to adolescence, the more frequently they will tell you the opposite! But as educators, we know that structure and predictability create safety, despite the grousing students may do about rules and being expected to abide by them.

Build success into every day

Students with trauma histories often have poor self-concept and a host of negative thoughts, including ones about their academic abilities (Jennings, 2018). Beyond that, homelessness often causes loss of school time, either through excessive absences or frequent school changes, which can lead to a loss of learning. Students consequently feel anxious about failing to measure up to their peers in the classroom, and they sometimes act out to distract themselves from these feelings, or to take teachers' attention away from their academic work. We can counteract this problem as teachers by making sure we create an opportunity in every lesson for struggling students to be successful, preferably publicly.

For example, in Kerri's first year of teaching, she had a second grader who, though not homeless per se, had only very recently arrived in the US after fleeing a violent civil war in her home country. We'll call her Francine, and she didn't speak English and had never been to formal school before. She was plopped in a classroom where no one shared her language or her culture, where everything from the food in the cafeteria to the styles of dress and interaction were different from what she'd known her whole life. Francine was experiencing quite a bit of trauma and her behaviors in the classroom belied this. With no words available, she used her fists to solve perceived disputes, and often wandered around the classroom during lessons. In addition to only gently correcting her behavior, never sending or referring her to the office, one strategy Kerri quicky adopted was to repeat the same question every morning until Francine could answer it. The class started each morning with students looking at a message Kerri had written to them on chart paper; it was the students' job to find and correct the "errors" she'd made. The types of errors varied (punctuation, spelling, etc.) but she always "forgot" to capitalize the first letter in her last name. It didn't take long until Francine was able to predict this, and even though that was 20 years ago, Kerri still remembers the smile on Francine's face the first time she raised her hand to answer "capital T in Tobin!" Kerri was then able to create different opportunities for her to have more success in front of her peers. Those moments when Francine not only felt competent but was able to demonstrate her skills to the class were crucial to her becoming a strong and confident student. She blossomed over the school year and went on to even greater success the next year, mastering reading in English in third grade.

Acknowledge feelings and don't use exclusion

While we're commonly taught to ignore small behaviors from students, so as not to allow every little thing to derail our teaching, traumatized students often need emotional validation to help themselves calm down. If a typically well-adjusted student gets frustrated and throws his paper on the floor, we can choose to ignore this behavior and assume the child will defuse and self-correct. But this is something we must assume a child who has experienced trauma cannot do alone. The same behavior from a student known (or suspected) to be experiencing a trauma like homelessness or abuse demands a different response. In cases like these, simple acknowledgement from the teacher can go a long way. Telling the student "it looks like you're frustrated with the assignment," without judgment or criticism, may help them feel seen and accepted.

Many of us also learned that it was appropriate to remove a problematic student from the rest of the class. For many children, this break can prove useful and can curb unwanted behaviors. But thanks to the explosion in research around trauma and the brain, we now know that sending a traumatized child to a desk at the back of the room, to the class next door, or to the office can trigger a cascade of emotional responses, particularly if that student has ever experienced abandonment or neglect. "We need to remember that when some of our students were young and cried, no one came. Ignoring them can trigger a trauma response and make them feel the teacher doesn't like them or is even happy that they are upset" (Minahan, 2019). It can be hard to shift our thinking this way, but the insights that we have into trauma and how it affects children's brains simply weren't available when most of us were training to be teachers. This knowledge can help us, and our students, now.

Teach about the brain and model self-calming strategies

The term social-emotional learning (SEL) has become popular in recent years as more and more schools and districts attempt to teach children how to navigate the world beyond academics. These programs aim to improve students' life skills like problem solving, self-control, and communication (Durlak et al., 2011). One crucial component of most good SEL programs gives students an age-appropriate understanding of the different regions of the brain, what they do, and what people can do to help those regions work in concert. Depending on the age of students in the classroom, science teachers can play a role in providing direct instruction using whatever level of technical terminology is approachable – an excellent example of this takes place in the documentary movie Paper Tigers (2015). For younger learners, one very popular approach is the "upstairs / downstairs brain" analogy: the "downstairs" brain (limbic system) is where feelings rule, while the "upstairs brain" (frontal cortex) is where thinking and reasoning are in control. If the downstairs brain makes all the decisions, we're acting on impulse, but when the upstairs brain is in charge, we are more likely to make choices based on evidence. Even very young children can be taught to understand that there are strategies we can use to "build a staircase" to connect these parts of our brains, or at least to improve communication between the two (Siegel & Bryson, 2011).

For self-calming strategies, younger children can be taught to take deep breaths, while older children may appreciate learning a little bit of the science behind blood oxygenation and why it makes us feel calmer. Basic strategies like counting to ten or tapping a rhythm on their own knee (quietly) in order to get control when emotions run amok can slow down students' reaction times and help them make decisions that do not get them into trouble. Meditation is another strong tool. Research in this area is new, but a 2020 study demonstrated that with 12 weeks of mindfulness training built into their school day, sixth graders' attention spans were significantly lengthened (Bauer et al., 2020). There are many mindfulness meditation programs for children, including the Calm app and the Annaka Harris website, which contains short but impactful (and free!) meditations suitable for use in the classroom.

Some children are particularly calmed by simple yoga movements, as they allow us to be in our bodies and to recognize the physical signs of distress that children may never have been taught, or permitted, to notice. Teachers can provide powerful learning by modeling their own processes of noticing their emotions, for example, "class, I can feel a headache coming on, this usually means I'm getting a little stressed," and how they deal with these signs, like "let's all take three deep breaths. Okay, I feel calmer now." Teachers can further model for students how the use of "I" statements give the speaker permission to have their own needs. For example, if a teacher feels students are crowding around her desk, "I need some personal space right now" is a much different statement than "move away from me." If we'd like our students to say things like the former when they speak to each other, we have to model that behavior ourselves. Children whose adult caretakers are preoccupied with finding housing or other forms of survival may not have seen healthy boundaries modeled in this way.

Learn more

If you are teaching a high number of students who have trauma in their lives, or if your community experiences a traumatic event that impacts everyone, such as a flood or a mass shooting, you can assume that your students with unstable housing will be more severely affected than their classmates. You might want to look into curricular approaches meant to create therapeutic environments that support all students. One example is the Support for Students Exposed to Trauma (SSET, 2021) program, which was designed by mental health professionals and intended for delivery by classroom teachers in late elementary through secondary grades. Its components include psychoeducation, relaxation and cognitive coping training, gradual exposure to trauma reminders, and problem solving (National Child Traumatic Stress Network, 2017). The entire curriculum is available online at no cost (see Jaycox et al., 2009). Even if you decide the whole program isn't feasible, you might decide to use some of its components.

Conclusions

Trauma cannot be cured by children themselves, and it is not the job of the classroom teacher to take on a task clearly meant for a mental health professional. But understanding that children's most challenging behaviors generally stem from stress or trauma – even if we don't know whether that trauma is homelessness or something else – and trying to build trusting relationships where students feel safe in the classroom, can help start students down a path to healing. Simple lessons about the brain, when coupled with easy-to-implement calming strategies, can create a sense of self-confidence for children whose emotions seem to get the best of them.

Chapter 6

What more can teachers do?

I feel very cheated as a teacher about a lot of things I've learned about with homelessness through the university so I'm not sure why they're not telling us this when we're the ones in the classroom. There's so many things we could easily do if we knew that they have a right to these services.

-Harper, first grade teacher

Unfortunately, as Harper notes, most teachers were not taught anything in their education courses about homeless students (California Research Bureau, 2007), and our own research findings lead us to predict that they will also not receive any professional development on the topic. But there are things teachers can do, and being aware that the population of students exists and has special needs and rights at school is a large part. Although the needs of this population can be as diverse as the living arrangements in which they find themselves, there are some overall recommendations we can make. In this chapter, we explore some other ways that teachers can support students experiencing homelessness. Although research on exact methods classroom teachers can use to support students experiencing homelessness is scarce, there are some common-sense approaches worthy of our attention.

Examine your perspective

In the United States, most teachers are white women from middle-class backgrounds (Taie & Goldring, 2020). Because of this, we often lack crucial similarities with the students we teach, as over 50% of public school students qualify for free and reduced lunch (Suitts, 2016) and 52% are students of color (National Center for Education Statistics, 2020b). It is important that we recognize the ways we may have internalized negative stereotypes about our students. Housing status is one of the ways students' experiences may be different from our own. Researchers have found that racial disparities in school discipline vary with county-level rates of racial bias (Riddle & Sinclair, 2019); it is possible that our internalized biases about how people come to be homeless might relate to how well our schools serve homeless students.

Although researchers have discovered that teachers often harbor negative ideas about parents experiencing homelessness – common stereotypes such as they are lazy or uninterested in their children's education – Powers-Costello and Swick found that "as teachers acquire more accurate information, they change their stance to become more positive and supportive" (2011). One important strategy for teachers is to surround ourselves with colleagues who believe in our students the way we do. Teachers can impact each others' thinking, so the people we sit with at lunch can frame how we respond to challenges in our classrooms.

> I feel like I learn which teachers are trying to be allies to the students, who are not approaching the job with a deficit mentality about the kids and only the things that they, you know, "cannot do." You just start to pick up on the teachers who have that perspective, and I lean on them a lot because it can be a pretty rough job. It can be an isolating job if you don't have those conversations.

-Matthew, 7th grade English teacher

Teachers sometimes forget the power we wield simply via our attitudes toward the children and families we work with (Kim, 2013). And we have most likely do have internalized prejudices, because everyone does. So how do we find out what they are, and how do we change them? If we empathize with our students we are able to be more effective teachers. If we are disdainful or judgmental, we cannot meet their needs. We can start by examining our thoughts about homelessness and what causes it, recognizing that many stably-housed people in the United States stigmatize people who experience homelessness. These prejudices can be seen in "general society, city legislation, law enforcement, and even the health care system" (De Las Nueces, 2016, p. 85). We don't need to beat ourselves up about the fact that we may harbor biases, however. We just need to take steps to change them. Reflection is the first step.

> [T]eachers construct their ideas about children and families from various factors present in their lives...the importance of teacher reflection about these experiences cannot be overstated as the reflective process holds great potential for empowering teachers to be more empathic with all children. (Powers-Costello and Swick, 2011, p. 208)

This is hard work, but teachers are not strangers to hard work. We can start by asking ourselves some difficult questions:

- Do I believe homeless families are somehow to blame for their own circumstances?
- Do I think parents experiencing homelessness are lazy?
- Do I think parents experiencing homelessness are bad parents?
- Do I think parents experiencing homelessness are uninterested in their kids' school success?

- Do I assume all adults experiencing homelessness suffer from substance use disorders and/or mental illness?

These questions may make us uncomfortable, but asking them is crucial. If we can understand our own perspectives, we can start to make changes that will benefit our students.

Collecting information is the next step. For example, reading about the affordable housing crisis in the United States can be eye-opening. Many middle-class people are unaware that, for example, the US has a dramatic shortage of affordable housing. Our nation has approximately 7.2 million more low-income families than affordable rental homes (Aurand et al., 2020). Likewise, many of us are surprised to learn that a third of parents experiencing homelessness do have jobs, but those jobs don't pay enough for them to afford housing (Applied Survey Research, 2018). Another statistic that can help us put homelessness into perspective is the role of violence in loss of housing: 57% of mothers cite domestic violence as the immediate cause for their homelessness (Family and Youth Services Bureau, 2016). Not only are these families without housing, but most experienced trauma in the process.

While these statistics can help us understand more about young children who are homeless with their families, it is also instructive to learn more about why adolescents, also called "unaccompanied youth," experience a loss of housing. Many of these young people are stereotyped as defiant runaways, just "bad kids" whose parents can't control them. Again, looking more closely gives us a very different picture. Youth generally leave home because home is dangerous for them – because they are being physically or sexually abused – or because they are told to leave. Very often, adolescents become unwelcome at home as the result of pregnancy or LGBTQ+ identification (Ingram et al., 2016). These students are extremely vulnerable, and it is not hard for us to understand why they might have issues trusting adults.

Beyond reading up about the reasons why children, youth, and families end up without housing, what else can a teacher do to shift her mindset? If possible, volunteer at or collect donations for your local family shelter. Work to cultivate respect and care for homeless children and their families by attending free webinars like those offered by SchoolHouse Connection, the nation's leading non-profit center for advocacy and resources for homeless education, the National Association for the Education of Homeless Children and Youth, or the National Center for Homeless Education. There are other ways to broaden your experiences, too. In much the same way that diversifying our media consumption can help reduce racial bias (Weisbuch et al., 2009), consuming popular media about people experiencing homelessness can help too. This list is not intended to be exhaustive, but just to give some ideas. Try to steer clear, however, of media that will reinforce stereotypes, particular the white savior trope present in movies like The Blind Spot.

Watch:
Movies: *The Florida Project* (2017); *Pursuit of Happyness* (2006)
Documentaries: *Children Underground* (2001)
                 Frontline: Poor Kids (2012 and 2017)
                 Homeless: The Motel Kids of Orange County (2010)
                 The Homestretch (2014)
                 Paper Tigers (2015)
                 Shelter (2016)

Listen:
Outsiders (Seattle Times, 2020)
Planet Money Episode 913: Counting the Homeless (NPR, 2019)
The Promise, Season 1 (Nashville Public Radio, 2018)
Solvable: Homelessness is Solvable (June 4, 2019)

Read:
Kozol, J. (1985) *Rachel and her children*
Desmond, M. (2016) *Evicted: Poverty and profit in the American city*
Elliott, A. (2013) *"Invisible Child: Dasani's Homeless Life."* New York Times.
Shapiro, E. (2019) *"114,000 Children in NYC Are Homeless. These Two Let Us Into Their Lives."* New York Times.

Beyond the ideas in this section, you can try to forge connections with families experiencing homelessness, though it is important to remember not to put any additional burdens on families already under extreme duress. If these relationships develop as part of your work to connect with and support families, they can help you increase your understanding of the experiences that accompany homelessness. But the onus is not on homeless families or children to educate teachers about their challenges. As Moore (2013), reminds us, "teachers should first understand their responsibility to identify and readjust their own misperceptions about students and families experiencing housing instability" (p. 4).

Be a detective

Once you're emotionally engaged and ready to support students, you can try to identify their living situations. This is as simple as a first-day-of-school assignment: "tell me about where you live." Kindergarteners can do this by drawing pictures, twelfth graders can do this in essay format. Amazing amounts of information can be gleaned with something low-stakes like this. Note that the assignment is not "tell me about your house/home," but rather "where you live." Teachers can also expand the assignment to include "tell me about who you live with." As noted in earlier chapters, experts believe that teachers have a crucial role to play in helping students who are experiencing homelessness. It can be frustrating when schools or districts choose to hide housing status information from teachers, but you can explore (sensitively) on your own.

    Obviously, information gathered in this manner should not be taken at face value. Students of all ages have myriad reasons for misrepresenting their lives, both to make them seem less dire (e.g., an unstably housed middle schooler might prefer to invent a house to tell the teacher about) or more unstable (e.g., a stably housed first grader may have seen or heard about homelessness and draw a picture of a family living in a car). But while this information should not be assumed to be factual, it can provide clues and things to look out for. If a student indicates an unstable living situation, you know you need to collect more information, either through conversation with the child (if you feel you have appropriate rapport), clues such as those listed in Chapter 2, or from other personnel at school.

Once you feel you have enough information to indicate a real concern about housing instability, the next step is to think about what to do with the information. Possibilities include: reaching out to parents/guardians listed on school paperwork, contacting the administration or front office staff, talking to your school counselor, or reaching out to the school social worker (if you have one). Unless you have reason to believe parents would feel comfortable disclosing potentially distressing information to you, and you'd be comfortable receiving it (more on this in Chapter 8), it's probably best to start with someone in your school – but it's important that you choose someone you trust. Miller et al. (2015) found that social workers often act as gatekeepers of students' housing status information, using what they perceive about teachers' trustworthiness when deciding whether to share the information.

Sometimes, a counselor or social worker will already know and may be able to confirm that the student is receiving services in accordance with McKinney-Vento. In these cases, the next step for a classroom teacher is to identify needs beyond what the law provides. For example, in Kerri's second grade class, one little girl who lived at the shelter didn't have sneakers for gym class, so she was not allowed to participate. Because she had the resources to do so, Kerri simply purchased a pair of sneakers for her and kept them in the classroom (because clothes and other items that went to the shelter unfortunately didn't seem to come back) so she could change into them before gym. Kerri also kept snacks in her desk drawer (what teacher doesn't?) and snuck something into the student's desk every morning so she could pull out a snack at snack time just like her classmates.

In many cases, though, teachers are already spending hundreds of dollars of their own money every year to supply their classrooms and students with the things they need to be successful, and we don't mean to imply that more of this will solve major, systemic problems. We suggest these only when feasible, and only as short-term stopgap measures for immediate problems. Your school may also have funds it uses for purposes like these, and many schools have relationships with local charities for supplies and donations – most of the teachers in our research indicate that their schools partner with specific local churches or organizations like the Salvation Army to provide children with necessities such as coats and canned food. Online fundraising options like GoFundMe and Donors Choose also provide ways for teachers to solicit donations for their classrooms. Charitable donations, like teachers' own money, should also not be seen as sensible solutions to huge societal problems like family homelessness (Aviles de Bradley, 2015), but they can help in the short term.

Choose curriculum and materials that affirm and support students' experiences

The mostly middle-class students in our elementary education courses often remark that they would not want to include any books or lessons about homelessness in their classrooms because they fear "triggering" or "traumatizing" students who are not stably housed. Unfortunately, though this impulse comes from concern for students' wellbeing, it is misguided. As long as you never reveal a child's housing status to his classmates, sensitive lessons and materials about homelessness can make the classroom a more welcoming and secure environment. Children who are experiencing homelessness know that they are experiencing homelessness. Teachers avoiding the subject does them no good. The benefits of these children seeing their own experiences affirmed and supported, as well as the benefits of raising their housed peers' awareness about homelessness, far outweigh the possibility that an unhoused child will be upset by a lesson focused on homelessness. All children deserve a classroom where they can discuss their living situations without fear of being stigmatized or shunned (Shields & Warke, 2010).

Housed children also need to learn about the experience of homelessness as one of the many variations of the human experience, even at young ages. Barnett, Quackenbush, and Pierce (1997) surveyed children and young adults and found that elementary students have more empathy for this population than older people. "[F]ourth graders generally expressed considerable concern for the homeless…and higher levels of sympathy/support for these individuals than did the high school and college participants" (p. 298). Not only is elementary school the ideal time to capitalize on and build students' capacity for empathy, students in this age group may also have misconceptions and fears that need to be unpacked and assuaged. There is also evidence that the way important adults – like teachers – behave influences children's behavior and attitudes toward helping others (e.g., Bryant & Crockenberg, 1980). We hold tremendous power to influence our students' feelings about those less materially fortunate than themselves, as well as their responsibility to contribute to the greater good.

A host of children's media exists to support teachers' attempts to normalize homelessness. Sesame Street has a character, Lily, who experiences homelessness. The website has videos, activities, and teaching resources. There's an episode of Reading Rainbow about homelessness available on Amazon Prime. Making purposeful choices for read-alouds or books to put in your classroom library can also help make homelessness something students are not afraid to talk about. For younger children, try Eve Bunting's *Fly Away Home*, Monica Gunning's *A Shelter in Our Car*, and Brenda Reeves Sturgess's *Still a Family.* For older elementary and middle schoolers, Katherine Applegate's *Crenshaw* is sensitive and thought-provoking. There are dozens of young adult novels about this topic, but *Pieces of Me* by Darlene Ryan and *Tyrell* by Coe Booth stand out.

Use targeted instructional approaches

Because we know that children experiencing homelessness often struggle with social connections, one of the strongest recommendations to come from the literature we reviewed in Chapter 3 is to create opportunities for cooperative work in the classroom. Obviously, groupwork is a strategy that teachers use for all students for a host of reasons, but remember it can be particularly helpful for students who have had to lose friends and may be hesitant about making new ones. These children are used to being disappointed by how their social relationships turn out (Duval & Vincent, 2009). However, it's also important to recognize that these students may not immediately be ready for groupwork. Putting a shy, withdrawn child with three or four classmates may intensify their feelings of awkwardness. Some students will need to be eased into cooperative work. Starting with short partner activities (like Think, Pair, Share in the elementary grades), students get practice using their voices and social skills with just one peer. With repeated success and comfort in this sort of activity, withdrawn or isolated students may soon become ready to work in a small group.

Another academic strategy that we alluded to in Chapter 3 is the idea of using strengths-based academic planning. This approach borrows from one of the foundational principles of the social work profession: the assumption that every individual has strengths, even if those strengths are not things traditionally valued at school (Saleebey, 2008). In education, we are often taught to see students the opposite way, in terms of the things they cannot do, their deficiencies and the places they struggle. The ubiquity of standardized benchmark testing and end-of-course assessments train us to focus on what students got wrong or demonstrated they do not know how to do. We call this a deficit model, one that looks at the shortcomings, or failings, of a student and then tries to fill in those gaps or fix the problem (Brownlee et al., 2012). One research team in Ontario, Canada, has worked to devise a system of assessing students' strengths through meetings with students and their parents, which then moves to a planning step where teachers use those strengths to build students' confidence and skills (Rawana et al., 2009). Even if teachers do not have access to parents or time to meet with every student in this way, there are standardized ways available to approach determining where students' strengths lie. Many schools are experimenting with administering a strengths-assessment survey or quiz to students, then using the results to motivate students (and teachers) to focus on what children already do well (Cornwall, 2018).

We previously discussed how students experiencing homelessness generally move residences and schools frequently, and this discontinuity can cause academic skill gaps to develop. Students themselves identify that teachers can help ease the stress around moving by offering extra help and materials (Begg et al, 2017). Another way teachers can help homeless and highly-mobile students is by making sure that, as often as possible, lessons start and end on the same day, or units start and end within the same week. This minimizes the chance that a student's learning of a particular concept or skill will be only partially complete if they have to move to a new school unexpectedly. Likewise, school records often get lost in the shuffle or are delayed when students switch schools. Teachers can provide written summaries of what students are studying each week, so that they (or their parents, for younger students) will have something to show to the next teacher. Fig. 3 shows an anonymized example of what this could look like (E. Perry, personal communication, March 22, 2021). It is a weekly newsletter sent to parents both electronically and in hard copy (in students' backpacks) that could easily be shared with a new teacher receiving a student at school mid-year and wondering what that student had been studying at their former school.

Ms. Perry's Class Newsletter
The Week of March 22 - 26

Learning Focus

SLA - We will be working on reading and spelling words with the letter b that makes the /b/ sound like bat. We will be focusing on the letters i, t, p, n, s, a, l, d, f, h, g, o, m, and b in cursive as well as building background for our next literature unit for the book "Bringing the Rain to Kapiti Plain" by Verna Aardema.

Math – We will finish up our graphing unit by creating and interpreting pictographs.

Social Studies Composition – We will continue our unit on famous American inventors and their impact on society. We will continue to learn to identify nouns and verbs by rearranging them to create sentences as well as the differentiating between statements, questions, and exclamations.

Science – We will continue our Earth science unit with learning about some different bodies of water.

Homework Schedule

Allow your child to continue to read aloud with you for 10 minutes every day (M-F) as part of their reading and sign off on the March tracker.

☺ Monday- ELA & Math Seesaw Activity

☺ Tuesday- Social Studies Composition & Science Activity

☺ Wednesday- ELA & Math Activity

☺ Thursday- ELA Activity & Work on Math Project

☺ Friday- Social Studies Composition & Science Activity

Teacher's Contact Info

Email: eperry@hypothetical.com

Testing Schedule

☺ **Monday—**
- **SLA:** Mini sub model & writing project due today ☺

Thursday—
- **Math:** Start working on your graded graphing project that will be due March 30th
- **SLA:** Graded spelling assessment

☺ **Friday—**
- **Science:** Graded Seesaw bodies of water assignment
- **Social Studies Composition:** Graded Seesaw writing assignment

** These testing dates are tentative and can be moved if the class is not prepared as seen fit by the teacher. **

Reminders

- There will be NO HOMEWORK next Friday!

- Be on the lookout Wednesday for a ParentSquare post from me to see if and what your child has earned as a Fun Friday reward this week since there will be no classes on Fridays.

- Please fill out the parent survey that was sent out on Parent Square for my class if you haven't done so already:

- Feel free to explore our virtual classroom with your child using the following link:

Figure 3: Sample classroom newsletter

Interestingly, Department of Defense (DoD) schools, which are attended by children whose parents are active in the United States military, serve a highly-mobile, low-SES population but have higher scores than traditional public schools. Researchers have sought to understand this for many years, and one of the components of DoD school success they have identified is the standardized curriculum – since all students in the same grade learn the same things at the same pace, there is little to no disruption in instruction when students have to change schools (Smrekar and Owens, 2003). Teachers know exactly what students learned at their previous school.

Address bullying head on

While bullying can affect students of all housing statuses, homelessness increases a student's likelihood of being the target of taunting and intimidation from peers. At both elementary and secondary levels, young people try to conceal their houselessness because it opens them up to judgement and often active harassment from their classmates. Sometimes the housing instability is obvious because of the transportation arrangements made by the school, or it is suspected because children's clothing doesn't get washed as often as their peers' does. Teachers must anticipate this and be ready to address it.

Conventional wisdom when many of us were young, or when we were training to become teachers, used to hold that bullies turned to that behavior because they themselves were bullied, or perhaps abused, at home. In recent decades, however, researchers have poked holes in this folk wisdom and discovered that while some bullies act out of retribution for a sense of powerlessness imposed upon them by their own tormentor, other children bully simply because it feels good. Psychologically healthy children sometimes just enjoy the feeling of power that comes with peers obeying their commands and catering to their whims (Swearer & Hymel, 2015). Researchers have also determined that the other folk wisdom, that kids should just ignore bullies, isn't likely to be successful either. What we now know is that the most powerful people in a bullying situation are actually the bystanders (Salmivalli & Voeten, 2004). Bullies aren't powerful without an audience, so newer curricula focus on empowering bystanders to intervene when they see bullying happening (see Welcoming Schools' What Can We Do? Bias, Bullies, and Bystanders video and lessons for kindergarten through eighth grade online). This is easiest to establish before a situation even starts, so that classrooms can be ready to welcome unstably-housed children at any point in the year.

Addressing bullying is obviously easier with younger children. Interventions really should start in preschool, since that is when we start to see bullying behavior, usually in the form of social exclusion, e.g., "you can't play with us" or "you can't sit here" take root. By the time students have reached middle and high school, teachers and schools can start to feel helpless because the problem is well-ingrained and bullying takes more complicated forms, especially with girls (Simmons, 2003). Many times, schools try interventions that run contrary to what research tells us is best practice. Things like peer mediation, once-a-year assemblies, and zero tolerance are all bad approaches to bullying that often make the situation worse. One assembly per year is not enough to effect any serious change. Peer mediation makes no sense; we don't take victims of spousal abuse and make them sit in a room with their abuser and a barely-trained non-professional to "mediate" as if each party were equally to blame. And zero tolerance actually makes victims and bystanders less likely to report bullying because they fear retaliation from the bully's friends. It's a complicated problem, but if nothing else, teachers can help by not ignoring bullying, much of which is based on perceived weakness or "other"ness like homelessness or LGBTQ+ identity (or both). We also need to be sure we don't fall into the trap of blaming the bullying victim. We sometimes seem to think that if victims of bullying ever try to stand up for themselves or try to fight back, that makes them somehow less deserving of victim status. A student need not sit passively and accept harassment in order to be a legitimate victim who deserves the teacher's help. Even if you can't solve bullying altogether, unhoused victims of bullying will feel safer and more supported if you acknowledge them and try to help.

Familiarize yourself with unaccompanied youth

While the focus of this work has been on children experiencing homelessness generally, we have tried to provide some examples and information specific to each of the two subpopulations: young children who are homeless with their families, and adolescents who are homeless all alone. Some of the experiences are similar. Both populations are likely to have trauma histories, for example, but some are different for the different groups. One way to be an effective educator of unaccompanied youth, those young people who have left or been told to leave home without any adult, is to familiarize yourself with the challenges that are specific to them.

The three sub-subpopulations

Unaccompanied youth become such for three main reasons, and researchers have given each group a term. "Runaway" youth are those who have run away from an unsafe or unwelcoming home, while "throwaway" youth have been told to leave. The third category of unaccompanied youth, referred to as "system youth," are young people who have been involved in government systems like juvenile justice or foster care (Tierney et al., 2008) and exited those facilities into homelessness. While each of these three groups has its own characteristics and challenges, there are a few commonalities to remember.

Unaccompanied youth are often considered to be even more vulnerable than young children experiencing homelessness with their parents. In addition to the somewhat obvious lack of an adult guardian in the lives of these young people, they are often suffering from multiple traumas: first and foremost, whatever precipitating event led to their separation from their family, and then the trauma of the separation itself. Youth run away from homes and foster homes where they have been victims of physical and sexual abuse, or they are rejected by their parents because they are gay or gender non-conforming. Pregnant and parenting teens are also likely to have been told to leave the family home. These young people then find themselves dealing with family rejection while trying to learn and survive life on the streets. They also often have to contend with discrimination based on their sexual identity, race, or parenting status at school and in agencies that provide mental and physical health care.

Victimization

Because they are alone, unaccompanied youth are at high risk for victimization, both physical and sexual, on the street (Jahiel, 1987). There is also evidence that many young people are forced to engage in what is termed "survival sex," or the exchange of sex for shelter, food, and other necessities (National Research Council, 2013), which leaves them vulnerable to victimization and sexually-transmitted infections (STIs). STIs, particularly HIV, affect homeless youth at high rates (Rew et al., 2005). LGBTQ+ youth are seven times more likely than heterosexual youth to have had to choose to trade sex for a place to stay, and 34% of cisgender female teens in one NYC study were trafficked, i.e., exploited by a third party for sex (Dank et al., 2015). Perhaps unsurprisingly, rates of suicidal ideation are very high for this group of homeless youth, higher than housed teens and higher than younger children who are unhoused but still with their parents (Hicks-Coolick et al., 2003). Despite all the risk factors present in their lives, however, unaccompanied youth have stores of strength and resilience much greater than we might imagine (Kidd & Davidson, 2007). They have learned to navigate complex and often dangerous worlds on their own, and when they do manage to show up to school, we should celebrate them.

Push back against dehumanizing policies

Students are supposed to wear navy blue jackets or sweatshirts when it gets cold. Every day she would come in with a new jacket that was wrong – a white one, a black one. She seemed to have this sort of endless supply of jackets that we would have to ask her to take off because they weren't in compliance with our uniform policy.

-Matthew, 7th grade English teacher

Pre-service teachers, often a bit starry-eyed, nearly always say that they have chosen to enter the profession because they love children or, in the case of secondary teachers, they love their subject matter. Even the most cynical might tell us that they find the school schedule appealing, but no one ever says "I want to be a teacher so I can fight with kids about their hoodies." Yet, somehow, enforcement of minor rules and guidelines ends up becoming incredibly common teacher behavior. For one thing, teachers sometimes see themselves as powerless not to participate in these actions, even taking a jacket away from a cold child because it's the wrong color. They believe their administrations will punish them – the teachers – for failing to enforce the school rules. They may also see themselves as sparing their students worse treatment by taking care of the problem before the student is "caught" by another teacher, or worse, a disciplinarian, who will enact a stronger punishment. But school policies not directly enhancing students' safety or learning are worthy of more interrogation by teachers.

Dress codes are perhaps the most problematic policies in this regard. Beyond being annoying for teachers, taking away precious instructional time, and enacting gender and racial bias (see, e.g., Aghasaleh, 2018; Edwards and Marshall, 2016), inflexible school dress code policies can cause a disconnect between students and school. For students who are struggling, particularly trying to escape the stigma of homelessness, being reprimanded daily for not having the right color shirt, or a belt, or the right color socks, can be disastrous. Policies like the one Matthew describes above, repeatedly forcing an undomiciled child to remove warm clothing because it's the wrong color, can seriously damage connections between the student and the school. A student in the scenario described above might reasonably conclude that school is not a hospitable place for her – she can't even be physically warm there – and choose to stop attending altogether. Could we blame her?

If you have autonomy in your classroom, think about policies like this. Research them. In the case of uniforms/dress codes, there is no conclusive evidence to show that they have a positive impact on behavior or academic performance (see, e.g., Baumann & Krskova, 2016; Bodine, 2003; Brunsma & Rockquemore, 1998). If you decide that a policy you're asked to enforce causes you to lose instructional time or damages your relationships with students, you might have the power to humanize your own space. When school cultures are hostile to children's needs, brave teachers can create oases of calm and safety behind their classroom doors. Are there minor infractions you can overlook in the name of students' emotional safety? If you choose to bend (or even ignore) some school rules in your classroom, think about how you'll explain your reasoning to your students, who will inevitably notice that you've chosen not to align yourself with all the stated school requirements. You may want to make sure you can bend the rules without damaging the authority of the school as a whole, or undermining your own authority by failing to align with the larger structure. Most students will understand and appreciate a teacher who refuses to enforce meaningless or harmful policies, but some will take such action as a sign of weakness and choose to try to exploit it. Also think about how you'll explain your reasoning to your school administration if asked. Having research at your disposal can be a good start.

In some schools, teachers are surveilled to make sure they spend time enforcing uniform policies. In these cases, changing expectations in your own classroom may not be possible. What can a teacher do in a situation like this one? First, make sure you're enforcing dress code rules in a fair and non-threatening way. This might mean being really introspective and self-critical to make sure you're enforcing the rules evenly across students. It also means you address violations in private, making sure not to embarrass the student. Even when students show us their worst selves, we cannot stoop to using humiliation to try to control their behavior.

This might also be a place to use pedagogy to make a point. When Kerri taught fourth grade, her students weren't allowed to go out to recess for weeks at a time because the recess aides determined it to be too cold outside and instead opted to pack the kids into the auditorium every day for yet another movie. The students grew restless, but there was not a lot Kerri could do to change this policy, so she turned it into a class assignment – the class researched school policies around the nation to learn what other schools considered "too cold" to go out for recess. The finished product was a memo to the principal using their research to back up a request to have the recess aides' policy changed. It was not successful, ultimately, but the students certainly knew their teacher was on their side. The same approach could go a long way toward building trust with students who are affected by other school policies over which the classroom teacher has no control. Ultimately, you as the teacher have to decide what hills you're willing to die on, so to speak, but remember that your students' safety is ultimately your responsibility.

Recognize the school's role

Uncomfortable as it may be for us to acknowledge, sometimes students' trauma happens at school, and we have to take ownership of this. Given all we presented in Chapter 5 about the negative impacts of trauma on a child, we need to make sure our schools and classrooms are not the sources of trauma for children, and that they don't compound trauma students have already suffered. Schools that take children's coats when they are cold, schools that misinterpret student behaviors and punish them harshly, schools that exclude them when what they – what all humans – want is to be included, to be safe, are places that can add to students' trauma or even cause it. Bullying, whether from peers or teachers/administrators, can amount to a trauma that further weighs on a student experiencing homelessness. Gaffney (2019) quotes a school trauma specialist who says, "I've seen children being embarrassed by the adults in their schools for not turning in homework or for talking too loudly in the hallway. That is violence toward kids." And she reminds us that this behavior on the part of adults at school "also reinforces the kind of dehumanizing treatment that many students receive from unjust structures out in the world – just for existing."

Schools that are culturally incompatible with students run the risk of causing real harm to them as well. Because most teachers are white and middle-class, they often cannot connect on a personal level with students' struggles. "Students of color and white students experience school differently" (Blitz et al., 2016, p. 97). The challenge for these teachers is to find strengths where they have been trained to perceive deficits, to see how students navigate and learn to survive in circumstances like homelessness and its attendant traumas. These teachers can then begin to build authentic relationships with students (Matias & Liou, 2015). One of the core principles of a trauma-responsive educator is the belief that when a group of students systematically underperforms on academic assessments, as is the case with homeless children, the problem lies with the school, not with the children (Silva et al., 2015).

Become the resource

Unfortunately, in most districts, information about how to support homeless students seems to be lacking (Ingram et al., 2016). Although teachers are already overtaxed, taking a few moments to locate resources you can give to students can be extremely helpful for them. It can also be helpful for you. Compassion fatigue, which will be discussed in more detail in the next chapter, can sap our energy and make us feel overwhelmed by the size of a problem like homelessness, but every small step we take goes a long way to alleviating our sense of hopelessness. Reflecting on her time teaching students who were not housed, Stephanie, a middle school teacher, noted

> I could've gone a little further out of the school, to go to the district to see if I could give [the student's] name…I could have just gotten some other resources to help them myself, community partners that may have been willing to help.

Another way teachers can support unhoused students is by encouraging them to attend school. Students may be reluctant to come to school in dirty clothes, or because the experience is stigmatizing. While teachers cannot singlehandedly solve all these problems, the simple act of acknowledging and celebrating students when they do manage to persevere through their circumstances and come to school can make them feel appreciated and seen. These feelings can lead to an increased desire to come to school. You can also reach out to parents to see what supports they think would help them get their children to school more reliably. Some school guidance counselors have gone as far as arranging a "buddy" family in the shelter to come and knock on the door in the morning and walk to school with a newer student. We need to think creatively about how we can get students to school and make them feel cared for when they get there.

Remember: You are an expert

While there is a bevy of research on the effects that housing instability has on children's educational outcomes, there is little that we know for sure about exactly what teachers should do to support these students. But as you've turned the pages of this book, you've probably thought of some good ideas already. You are an expert in teaching and learning. Use your creativity and apply what you know about best teaching practices to engage with homeless students. Try different approaches and methods until you find something that works for your classroom style and the needs of your specific students.

> I had a mentor teacher…what he does is after school get [an unstably house child] a worksheet, couple worksheets at a time, and stay after school with him. Take time, help him with the worksheet, because when you single them out, they tend to shut down. And when he does good, congratulate him: good job, keep up the good work. Because what that does is encourage them and boost their self-esteem.

-Stephen, 8th grade teacher

Even though Stephen's mentor teacher's approach isn't one that has been researched extensively, it contains many of the elements of good practice we've discussed here. He knew intuitively to work on students' self esteem and to take things slowly. What developed was, no doubt, a successful approach that led to his undomiciled students feeling seen and cared for.

Chapter 7

What is compassion fatigue and how can we avoid it?

Empathy, the ability to put ourselves in other people's shoes and understand how they are feeling, is an important trait for teachers. It makes us responsive to our students' needs. It makes us care about their emotional lives and lets them know they are cared for. But there can be a downside to our empathy, and that is when we become overwhelmed by the depth or breadth of our students' suffering. In psychology, there is a phenomenon known as the "scope-severity paradox," which explains how when we see one person suffering, our heartstrings are tugged and we are energized to help them. But as the number of people suffering increases, our ability to imagine how we can make a difference decreases (Loewenstein, 1996). And when we feel like we can't possibly make a difference, we stop feeling compassionate. Our minds want to protect us from feeling helpless, so we start trying to create distance, even subconsciously, from the people we care for. Teachers are incredibly important not only in their capacity as deliverers of content knowledge but also in establishing caring and supportive classrooms where students can develop emotionally (Weston et al., 2008). Overwhelming situations that lead teachers to distance themselves are present in many unhoused students' backgrounds, so we need to know how to protect our capacity to help.

Compassion fatigue

When teachers start to feel exhausted, cynical, and sometimes even depressed or traumatized ourselves, this is known as *compassion fatigue*. The term was first coined by Figley (1995) in an attempt to organize psychologists' experiences with people who had not been directly exposed to a traumatic situation but had nonetheless experienced a form of trauma from it; he also called it *secondary traumatic stress disorder*. It can be thought of as "the natural consequent behaviors and emotions resulting from knowing about a traumatizing event experienced by a significant other—the stress resulting from helping or wanting to help a traumatized or suffering person" (Hydon et al., 2015, p. 320). Although Figley originally created the term to describe the experiences of people whose own family members had been traumatized, he quickly expanded it when he discovered that other mental health professionals saw the same reactions in employees in the so-called helping professions like medicine, social work, and education.

When we are confronted over and over with the suffering of others whose problems we can't fix, especially when the victims of that suffering are people we care about, we get overtaxed and run out of energy. If we care about our students, but our students are suffering, we may start to suffer too. We may feel overwhelmed and start to shut down emotionally. When our empathy is drained to the point where we become emotionally numb, we're suffering from compassion fatigue. Basically, it becomes too exhausting, both emotionally and sometimes physically, to feel compassionate anymore. We might give in to feelings of hopelessness or become jaded and cynical. Teachers who work with students who have been or are experiencing traumas like homelessness outside school are susceptible to compassion fatigue. "Teachers frequently become attached to the children they teach, in turn, experiencing distress when they witness daily reminders of the hardships these children face at home, including abuse, neglect, divorce, household danger, and poverty" (Hupe & Stevenson, 2019, p. 3).

> You want to be attached to all the kids, but you really can't. You really can't. So when…you don't see them for a couple of days, you wonder what's going on. Have they moved to another school? Have they moved to another state, another city?

-Sheila, 4th grade teacher

Working with children who experience extremely challenging circumstances, particularly when a large number of them seem to face insurmountable obstacles, can lead to compassion fatigue. Sheila, above, notes that "you really can't" get attached to "all" the kids, because in her school, there are too many, and the experience of getting attached and then losing contact with students she cared for grew too painful for her. Her comments indicate that she has grown weary over the years. Caring about others takes time and energy, which are unfortunately finite resources. People at high risk for compassion fatigue include "those working directly with traumatized individuals…those who tend to be empathetic, females…and those helping professionals who have unresolved histories of trauma themselves" (Hydon et al., 2015, p. 320).

Unfortunately, when we stop caring, our students suffer. In extreme cases, compassion fatigue has been demonstrated to reduce the likelihood that teachers will report suspected cases of child abuse. In one study, 11% of teachers found to be suffering compassion fatigue admitted that they had suspected students were being abused but had not reported it (Kenny, 2001). Although we devoted some time in Chapter 5 to critique of the foster care system and child protective services in the United States, teachers are still mandated reporters and if they truly believe children are being harmed, they are supposed to report this information to the appropriate authorities. Children's safety should be our primary concern. But some teachers get to the point where they are too overwhelmed to take action even when they fear for a student's safety.

Vicarious trauma

Another phenomenon related to compassion fatigue is *vicarious trauma* (Perlman & Saakvitne, 1995) – vicarious means we live the trauma through someone else describing it. It is very similar to Post-Traumatic Stress Disorder, which most of us know as PTSD and often associate with veterans or victims of violent crimes. The official PTSD diagnosing criteria note that it can be caused by "indirect exposure to aversive details of the event(s), usually in the course of professional duties" (American Psychiatric Association, 2013, p. 271). Hearing about the trauma our students suffer outside of school, from homelessness to abuse to displacement, can trigger a similar response in us (Sizemore, 2016). Since students often disclose details about their home lives, teachers are likely to be exposed to secondary trauma (Hill, 2011).

> So we have to be very careful when inquiring about their living circumstances. [Sometimes] they'll admit they've lost their home, or they've been evicted, or they've had to move because they don't have a car to get to school or to work. It's…it's very disheartening. We gave some clothes to a young girl this afternoon…it's ok because we'd rather take care of her than make her feel like she was incapable of caring for herself. And that's not an easy thing cause you want to build some kind of confidence in kids – not make 'em feel like they can't buy a shirt or pair of pants or…sorry. I'm gonna start crying because I'm just thinking about that sweet little thing today.

-Harper, first grade teacher

Additionally, when a traumatic event affects a whole community, like an act of violence or a natural disaster, students already dealing with challenges outside of school (like housing instability) may be affected more greatly than their class-mates. And when teachers are directly impacted by the event themselves, rela-tionships can become further complicated. For example, in Southeast Louisiana, where we live and work, the shadows of unresolved trauma histories loom large in the form of environmental disaster: Hurricane Katrina reshaped the landscape of New Orleans in 2005, and Baton Rouge saw catastrophic flooding in 2016. In such cases as these, when teachers are exposed to their students' suffering and also directly affected themselves, some may be overwhelmed. But the possibility also exists that the teacher's empathy may be strengthened. One student teacher whose family was displaced by the Baton Rouge flood of 2016 found that she was actually better able to sympathize with students who were in similar situations; their shared trauma giving her insight into how her students were feeling. When the class came to an instructional unit on the role of flooding in civilizations of the ancient river valleys, this novice teacher was on high alert and able to recognize that she would need to present the material very carefully to avoid further trau-matizing her students. "How was I supposed to explain silt and the flooding of the Nile when my students had gutted silt-covered items from their own homes?" (Spears, 2017, p. 45)

Protecting yourself

In order for teachers to work effectively with children who are being punished "for the sins of our economic and social policies" (Love, 2020, p. 1), we need to find ways to protect ourselves from vicarious trauma, compassion fatigue, and burnout.

> [T]hings that take place at home that you can't help, but it comes to school. And they're just too young to go through that or understand it, and you can only say so much without getting into their personal business…I'm not their parent so I don't want to overstep those bounds. But that is challenging.

> -Sallie, elementary music teacher

Sallie's approach here indicates that she is aware of students' challenges but she is also aware of the limitations of what she can do as a teacher and not their parent. Maintaining boundaries like this, reminding ourselves what we can and cannot do, but working hard to do all the things that are appropriate, may help to stem the tide of compassion fatigue.

Signs and Symptoms

It can be difficult to determine whether you are experiencing compassion fatigue or secondary traumatization from absorbing the traumas your student experience, but it is possible you may experience some of the following symptoms:

- difficulty talking about your feelings
- free floating anger and/or irritation
- startle effect/being jumpy
- low motivation
- difficulty falling asleep and/or staying asleep
- worry that you are not doing enough for your students
- diminished feelings of satisfaction and personal accomplishment
- feelings of hopelessness associated with your work/your students
- withdrawal and isolation from colleagues
- apathy and/or detachment
- pushing yourself too hard, trying to do everything yourself

(*Adapted from American Counseling Association,* 2011 and Hydon et al., 2015))

If you notice that one or more of these resonate with you, the National Center on Safe and Supportive Learning Environments (NCSSLE, 2021), a project of the United States Department of Education, recommends the following steps: 1) be aware of the signs; 2) reach out to others, like your colleagues, for support; 3) recognize that compassion fatigue is not a sign of weakness or that something is wrong with you; 4) seek help with your own traumas; and 5) talk to a mental health professional. The NCSSLE also offers webinars and curricular resources on its website. The usual recommendations of self-care to treat more generalized stress may not be sufficient to help with vicarious trauma or compassion fatigue.

Although most schools and districts do not offer comprehensive employee wellness programs, the Directors of Health Promotion and Wellness (DHPE, 2005) has created a guide for school leaders on what a successful program would look like.

- Health education and health-promoting activities that focus on skill development and lifestyle behavior that change along with awareness building, information dissemination, and access to facilities and preferably are tailored to employees' needs and interests
- Safe, supportive social and physical environments, including organizational expectations about healthy behaviors and implementation of policies that promote health and safety and reduce the risk of disease
- Integration of the worksite program into the school or district structure
- Linkage to related programs such as employee assistance programs, emergency care, and programs that help employees balance work and family life
- Worksite screening programs, which ideally are linked to medical care to ensure follow-up and appropriate treatment as necessary
- Individual follow-up interventions to support behavior change
- Education and resources to help employees make decisions about health care
- An evaluation and improvement process to help enhance the program's effectiveness and efficiency (DHPE, 2055, p. 1)

While most of us cannot even imagine such a program existing to support teachers, these are best practices that experts recommend. At the very least, recognizing that we are working without those ideal supports, and in many cases with no supports at all, should allow us to be compassionate with ourselves. Teachers are doing difficult jobs in suboptimal conditions, but there are resources.

- The United States Department of Health and Human Services lists some research-supported strategies for battling compassion fatigue on their website. These include mindfulness, creative expression, work-life balance, and seeking professional help (Administration for Children and Families, 2021).
- Research supports the effectiveness of teacher peer support groups (Lander, 2018).
- Learning for Justice has a toolkit that includes a self-assessment tool for professionals who work with traumatized children, as well as resources to build your own resilience (Learning for Justice, 2015).
- Perhaps the best resource is a program called Support for Teachers Affected by Trauma (https://statprogram.org), developed by experts to raise awareness in teachers about how their students' trauma impact them and how to manage its effects.

Teacher stress and burnout

While compassion fatigue is not the same thing as burnout, it can lead to burnout, a disenchantment with work that happens over time (American Counseling Association, 2011). Burnout can happen in any profession and refers to a point where employees experience exhaustion at or when thinking about work, become less engaged in their work, and may experience feelings of dread or disillusionment about working (Mayo Clinic, 2021). Burnout generally happens as a result of long-term exposure to a stressful working environment, often one where tasks come from a place outside our control, need to be done constantly, and demand to be done more quickly than we feel is possible. Does this sound familiar? It describes teaching for a lot of us. Teachers experience high levels of stress with low levels of administrative support (OECD, 2014). Once again, being in a helping profession like education is a risk factor for job burnout. Likewise, in our own research, we find that women are more likely to express sympathy for people experiencing homelessness, indicating that for whatever reason, women may be more in tune to others' emotional needs and also more likely to absorb their stresses.

Teacher stress can lead to burnout, and it has been the subject of research study for over 20 years. Teachers have difficult jobs and the profession has a high turnover rate (Gray & Taie, 2015). Almost half of teachers report high levels of daily stress (Lever, 2017) and research has identified two main areas that contribute to it: excessive workload and student behavioral challenges – a term that encompasses students' externalizing or internalizing responses to their trauma, and leads to less effective teaching (Collie et al., 2012). Interestingly, teachers report less stress when they know that their students can access mental health treatment outside of the classroom (Ball & Anderson-Butcher, 2014). Something about knowing they are not solely responsible for supporting their students' mental health seems to ease their own suffering and feelings of stress.

Getting attached

Whether from compassion fatigue, stress, or a desire to protect themselves from being hurt, teachers often fail to make meaningful connections with students who enter their classrooms after the start of school (or who they expect will leave before the year ends).

> It's hard to build a relationship with a kid when they don't come at the beginning of the year to begin with. And…so you work really hard to build that relationship with them, you know, outside of your normal context in which you do that which is at the beginning of the year, and a lot times right about the time that I feel I've sort of broken through and I have a good relationship and there's some trust established, they're gone again.

-*Matthew, 7th grade English teacher*

The situation Matthew describes sounds very frustrating, because he has put time into a relationship and he will likely never know the outcome of the time he invested. He extended himself emotionally but may never get to see the fruits of that labor. While it's understandable to feel this way, we need to remember that kindnesses we show to students now may very well enhance their well-being both immediately and down the line, even if we're not there to see it.

> [School personnel] asked "how long are they gonna be here?" And I said, "Well, we don't know. But they don't have anywhere else to go right now, so…"

-Jeanne, Homeless Education Administrator

Losing contact with students we care about, especially with no warning, can be very emotionally taxing, but we can mitigate that by trying, early on, to connect students with other sources of support as we support them ourselves. This both reduces the burden we have to carry, because we know they can turn to other trusted adults, and builds their capacity to trust others and form connections of their own, skills that will serve them well after they've left our classrooms.

> Because you'll get attached to a student, and then they are taken away. You know… and you'll see the potential in them. It's just that they can't help it because they're not an adult. So they have to what an adult tells them to do, especially their parents. "Wherever my parent goes, I have to go because I can't take care of myself." So it's kind of hard.

-Megan, 3rd grade teacher

Megan provides valuable insight here as well – students have no control over whether they stay in our classes all year or not. But it may nonetheless still hurt when they leave. "The student simply disappears from class. This can be stressful for both the student and the teacher" (Hallett & Skrla, 2017, p. 14).

> One child who told me she was homeless…I referred her to guidance and they were able to find her a place to live, and then after that I didn't know what happened to her.

-Robin, high school teacher

Behavior issues

Perhaps the biggest problem for teachers is when students' trauma leads to unpredictable behavior in the classroom. Classroom management struggles are one of the main factors that lead to teacher stress and burnout (Lever et al., 2017). Teachers may experience students as overreactive to peer interactions, explosive, even openly defiant. If we don't recognize these behaviors as trauma responses and try to address them with compassion and consistency, the situation is unlikely to improve. And when teachers don't know what to expect from students, "uncertainty leaves the teacher in a constant state of hyper-alertness when interacting with the student. This in turn can result in fatigue, as the teacher is guarded and unable to predict what will happen from one moment to another" (Minahan, 2019). Here we can see how the student's responses to an unpredictable life can cause the exact same lack of predictability for the teacher.

In situations like these, our best bet is to stay alert for signs and symptoms in ourselves when classroom behavior is hard to manage. When we recognize that we are being profoundly affected, we can try trauma-responsive strategies. If these do not work, we need to find compassionate mental health providers to assist us in our work of making school safe for our student(s) and ourselves. Our levels of compassion fatigue and burnout affect our students' learning. Researchers have linked teacher burnout with lower motivation and less effective teaching (Zhang & Sapp, 2008). And our mental health may actually cause stress for students: one study identified that teachers' levels of burnout correlated with the cortisol in their elementary students' bodies (Oberle & Schonert-Reichl, 2016).

Conclusions

Even though we know that teaching is a stressful occupation, and research shows that employee wellness programs are beneficial in preventing burnout, only 25% of schools offer stress management programming for staff (Lever et al., 2017). We also know that teachers tend to be empathetic and caring, which unfortunately leaves them vulnerable to absorbing their students' traumas. This in turn can lead to compassion fatigue, a state where teachers start to feel numb and distance themselves from their highest-need students. Unfortunately, burnout is also common in the profession. While 89% of new teachers are enthusiastic about their jobs, that number is a startlingly low 15% for veteran educators (Gray & Taie, 2015). Birmingham (2009) believes that many teachers travel "a path on which the energized idealism of a hope-filled teacher distorts into the jaded cynicism of a teacher defeated" (p. 33). None of us entered teaching hoping to become burned out or fatigued, but these are common experiences. Especially when we work with traumatized populations like students experiencing homelessness, we need to stay alert for signs that we may be experiencing compassion fatigue and take action when we do.

Chapter 8

Where do we go from here?

While what is presented in this volume might feel overwhelming, or like another set of things to add to a teacher's ever-lengthening list of responsibilities, we want to end on a note of hopefulness. First, by reading this book, you've become more aware and are now part of the solution. Second, you have tools to help support your houseless students and ideas about where to go to find (and create) more. And third, you know more about how to protect yourself from compassion fatigue and burnout so you can stay in the classroom and keep making a difference in the lives of children, especially those placed in the most vulnerable positions like homelessness.

There is also some good news to consider. Though it's difficult to see an upside to the Covid-19 crisis, public awareness of homelessness has been on the rise, and we may see policies enacted that provide more support to these vulnerable individuals and families. States have begun to make headway in how they serve homeless youth as well. True Colors United, an organization that advocates for policies that support homeless LGBTQ+ youth, releases an annual report that ranks the states on how their laws and budgetary decisions affect these vulnerable young people. In the most recent report (Waguespack & Ryan, 2020), not only was Washington, DC was the first jurisdiction in the history of the report to earn an A grade for their support of youth experiencing homelessness, but all 50 states improved their service delivery over the past year. Advocates are raising awareness of the needs of homeless youth and families, and we will continue to see improvements in how states and cities allocate funds and services to support them.

Hope

One of the best tools we can bring to the classroom when we teach students experiencing homelessness is hope. This may sound obvious or it may sound vague. What do we mean by hope, exactly? Hope can be defined as "an overall sense that one's goals can be met" (Snyder, 2005, p. 61), which is a feeling that humans need in order to live successful lives. We need to have a sense of hope that things will work out, that we will be safe and have our needs met. When we have it, we can make the most of our circumstances and envision a positive future for ourselves. "Hopefulness is a human characteristic that allows an individual, irrespective of age, to transcend disappointments, pursue goals, and diminish the sense of future as unbearable or futile" (Herth, 1998, p. 1054). It is not hard to imagine, however, how a life filled with traumas like family dysfunction or homelessness might leave children bereft of such a belief that their lives will work out okay or that things will get better (Weinger, 1998). Indeed, in their study of the experiences of homeless third through sixth graders, Begg and colleagues found that homeless children struggle to develop a "positive personal narrative" (p. 238) because their experience is both stigmatized and marginalized – the dominant idea we have about a what constitutes a good childhood generally includes staying in one school, getting good grades, and being able to rely on parents to provide basics like housing and food, which are things homeless students often cannot do. These things can lead to a loss of sense that things will turn out well for them. "Hope can be destroyed," Birmingham warns us (2007, p. 27).

However, whereas homeless children might reasonably experience hopelessness, some studies have found the opposite. Herth (1998) interviewed children at an emergency shelter and found that their sense of hope was alive and well when they were asked to draw and then talk about what hope means to them. She also found that hope has two elements: a core belief that life will turn out well in a general sense, plus tendrils of secondary, more specific hopes for particular outcomes, like good grades or stable housing. "All of the children, irrespective of age, were able to identify what was hopeful in their lives and felt that hope was absolutely essential despite their expressed distress about the constant disruptions and lack of stability in their lives" (Herth, 1998, p. 1057). Something nurtured the children's hope (Birmingham, 2009), supporting Lynch's (1965) assertion that hope can be learned. Previous research had demonstrated that the same could happen for homeless mothers: when they were surrounded by caring people, they flourished and expanded their capacity to believe that better things were possible (Baumann, 1994).

Percy (1995) found that children in a homeless shelter experienced fun and a feeling that they were cared for despite their overwhelmingly dire circumstances. She postulated that laughter and having fun may buffer stress in resilient children. But what does it mean to be a resilient child? The fields of child development and psychology have come together over the last three decades to examine why some children are able to be successful despite terrible circumstances, while others are not so resilient. Masten and her team, foundational researchers in this area, found that children who face difficult circumstances "fare better or recover more successfully when they have a positive relationship with a competent adult, they are good learners and problem-solvers, they are engaging to other people, and they have areas of competence and perceived efficacy" (1990, p. 425). We talked in Chapter 6 about how to engender a sense of competence by using student strengths and creating opportunities for them to feel successful. Studies since then have also replicated the finding that children are more likely to be able to transcend difficult circumstances if they have even one significant adult in their lives who can be trusted and relied upon. A teacher is often perfectly positioned to be that person. Begg and her team (2017) found that homeless children identify role models when talking about their successes and their hopes for the future. The children in Herth's (1998) study often named their teachers as significant role models, and it is likely that these teachers were instrumental in helping children retain "an inner strength that rekindled their hope even in the worst of situations" (p. 1058).

Maintaining our own hope

In order for teachers to become people who help their unhoused students sustain or re-learn a sense of hope, is teachers ourselves have hopefulness in our own lives. Teaching can be a profession where it is hard to have hope. Teachers have to live with uncertainty about whether their actions will lead to good results for their students in the long term (Van Manen, 2000), so they do not always get the reinforcement that lets them know their efforts are successful. But hope does not require the desired outcome to be likely, only possible (Birmingham, 2009). We do not have to believe that all our actions will lead our students to happy lives after they leave our classes, only that it could happen. Remembering this can also help the way we behave and the decisions we make in the classroom. Imagine a scenario in which a student comes to school in a bad mood. Do you steel yourself for inevitable bad outcomes? Or do you hold onto the possibility that things could turn around?

> If a student arrives to class in a pessimistic and irritable mood, his teacher can still hope that this student will have a good day of learning and getting along with his classmates, for hope does not require that the teacher believes the student will have a good day. (Birmingham, 2009, p. 30)

Even though we know, and research demonstrates, that teachers may lose their sense of hope over the years, because the job is so taxing (Estola, 2003), a simple shift in the way we view our jobs may help. We may not be successful at getting every one of our students into Harvard, but as long as our actions do not remove the possibility, we are operating from a hopeful perspective and encouraging our students to do the same. Baumann (1993) reminds us that the best way to inspire our students, especially those struggling with challenges like homelessness, is to be present for them. "True presence is a way of being with the children that is attentive, open, nonjudgmental, and genuinely respectful of the child's becoming" (p. 60). Most of us entered the teaching profession believing that "children of all minority and oppressed groups can learn as well as those of the privileged and dominant classes" (Noddings, 1993, p. 730), and while we may need to reconnect with that sentiment on occasion, we will almost always find that it is still there.

References

Abel, J. and Deitz, R. (2014). Do the benefits of college still outweigh the costs? *Current Issues in Economics and Finance*, (20), 3. Federal Reserve Bank of New York. https://www.newyorkfed.org/medialibrary/media/research/current_issues/ci20-3.pdf

Aber, L., Bennett, N. G., Conley, D. C., & Li, J. (1997). The effects of poverty on child health and development. *Annual Review of Public Health*, 18, 463–483.

Administration for Children and Families. (2021). *Secondary Traumatic Stress. Washington, DC: United States Department of Health and Human Services.* https://www.acf.hhs.gov/trauma-toolkit/secondary-traumatic-stress

Aghasaleh, R. (2018). Oppressive curriculum: Sexist, racist, classist, and homophobic practice of dress codes in schooling. *Journal of African American Studies*, 22, 94-108.

Alaimo, K., Olson, C., and Frongillo, E. (2001) Food insufficiency and American school-aged children's cognitive, academic, and psychosocial development. *Pediatrics*, 108(1), 44- 53.

Alperstein, G., Rappaport, C., and Flanigan, J. (1988) Health problems of homeless children in New York City. *American Journal of Public Health*, 78, 1232-1233.

American Counseling Association. (2011). *Fact Sheet #9: Vicarious Trauma.* https://www.counseling.org/docs/trauma-disaster/fact-sheet-9---vicarious-trauma.pdf

Aerican Psychiatric Association. (2013). *Diagnostic and Statistical Manual of Mental Disorders.* 5th ed. Arlington, VA: American Psychiatric Association.

Anderson, L., Janger, M., & Panton, K. (1995). *An Evaluation of State and Local Efforts to Serve the Educational Needs of Homeless Children and Youth.* Washington, DC: U.S. Department of Education, Office of Educational Research and Improvement.

Anoosihan, L. (2005). Violence and aggression in the lives of homeless children: A review. *Aggression and Violent Behavior* (10)2, 129-152.

Applied Survey Research. (2018). *San Francisco Homeless Count & Survey 2017: Comprehensive Report.* Watsonville, CA: Author.

Aratani, Y. (2009). *Homeless Children and Youth: Causes and Consequences.* New York, NY: National Center for Children in Poverty.

Ardoin, S. (2017). *College aspirations and access in working-class, rural communities: The mixed signals, challenges, and new language first-generation students encounter.* Lexington Books.

Aupperle, R. L., Melrose, A. J., Stein, M. B., & Paulus, M. P. (2012). Executive function and PTSD: Disengaging from trauma. *Neuropharmacology*, 62(2), 686–694.

Aurand, A., Emmanuel, D., Threet, D., Rafi, I., and Yentel, D. (2020). *The Gap: A Shortage of Affordable Homes.* Washington, DC: National Low-Income Housing Coalition.

Aviles de Bradley, A. (2015). *From Charity to Equity: Race, Homelessness, and Urban Schools.* New York, NY: Teachers College Press.

Baby's First Years. (2021). *Study Background.* https://www.babysfirstyears.com/about

References

Ball, A., & Anderson-Butcher, D. (2014). Understanding teachers' perceptions of student support systems in relation to teachers' stress. Children & Schools, 36(4), 221-229.

Barnes, A., Gilbertson, J., and Chatterjee, D. (2019). Emotional health among youth experiencing family homelessness. Pediatrics, 141(4).

Barnett, Quackenbush, & Pierce. (1997). Perceptions of and reactions to the homeless: A survey of fourth-grade, high school, and college students in a small Midwestern community. Journal of Social Distress and the Homeless, 6(4), 283-302.

Bassuk, E., & Beardslee, W. (2014). Depression in homeless mothers: Addressing an unrecognized public health issue. American Journal of Orthopsychiatry, 84(1), 73–81.

Bassuk, E., DeCandia, C., Beach, C., & Berman, F. (2014). America's youngest outcasts: A report card on child homelessness. Waltham, MA: National Center on Family Homelessness.

Bassuk, E. and Rosenberg, L. (1990) Psychosocial characteristics of homeless children and children with homes. Pediatrics, 85, 257-261.

Bassuk, E. and Rubin, L. (1987). Homeless children: A neglected population. American Journal of Orthopsychiatry, 57, 279-286.

Bauer, C., Rozenkrantz, L., Caballero, C., Nieto-Castanon, A., Scherer, E., West, Mrazek, M., Phillips, D., Gabrieli, J., & Whitfield-Gabrieli, S. (2020). Mindfulness training preserves sustained attention and resting state anticorrelation between default-mode network and dorsolateral prefrontal cortex: A randomized controlled trial. *Human Brain Mapping*, 41(18), 5356-5369.

Baumann, C., & Krskova, H. (2016). School discipline, school uniforms and academic performance. *International Journal of Educational Management*, 30(6), 1003-1029.

Baumann S. (1994). No place of their own: an exploratory study. *Nursing Science Quarterly* 7(4), 162-169.

Baumann S. (1993). The meaning of being homeless. *Scholarly Inquiry for Nursing Practice: An International Journal* 7(1), 59-73.

Begg, N., Levitt, M., & Hayden, A. (2017). Understanding the school experience of African-American homeless children. *Journal of Constructivist Psychology*, 30(3), 235-254.

Beharry, M. (2012). Health issues in the homeless youth population. *Pediatric Annals*, 41(4), 154-156.

Better Homes Fund. (1999). *Homeless children: America's new outcasts*. Newton, MA: Author.

Birmingham, C. (2009). The disposition of hope in teaching. *Teacher Education Quarterly*, 36(4), 27-39.

Blitz, L., Yull, D., and Clauhs, M. (2016). Bringing sanctuary to school: Assessing school climate as a foundation for culturally responsive trauma-informed approaches for urban schools. *Urban Education*, 55(1), 95-124.

Bodine, A. (2003). School uniforms, academic achievement, and uses of research. *Journal of Educational Research*, 97(2), 67-71.

Bonagura, R. (2008). Redefining the baseline: Reasonable efforts, family preservation, and parenting foster children in New York. *Columbia Journal of Gender and Law*, 18(1).

Books, S. (2004). *Poverty and schooling in the U.S.: Contexts and consequences*. Mahwah, NJ: Erlbaum.

Bourdieu, P. (1973). *Cultural reproduction and social reproduction in knowledge, education and cultural change*. London: Tavistock.

Boxhill, N., and Beaty, A. (1990) Mother/child interaction among homeless women and their children in a public night shelter in Atlanta, Georgia. In Boxhill, N. (Ed.), *Homeless Children: The watchers and the waiters* (pp. 49-64). London: Haworth Press.

Bowman, D., Burdette, Julianelle, P. (2008). *Homeless and Special Education Administrative Collaboration: Recommendations*. Alexandria, VA: National Association of State Directors of Special Education.

Brownlee, K., Rawana, E. P., & MacArthur, J. (2012). Implementation of a strengths-based approach to teaching in an elementary School. *Journal of Teaching and Learning*, 8(1).

Brunsma, D. L., & Rockquemore, K. A. (1998). Effects of student uniforms on attendance, behavior problems, substance use, and academic achievement. *Journal of Educational Research*, 92(1), 53-62.

Bryant, B. K., & Crockenberg, S. B. (1980). Correlates and dimensions of prosocial behavior: A study of female siblings with their mothers. *Child Development*, 51, 529-544.

Buckner, J. (2008). Understanding the impact of homelessness on children. *American Behavioral Scientist*, 51(6), 721-736.

Buckner, J., Bassuk, E., and Weinreb, L. (2001) Predictors of academic achievement among homeless and low-income housed children. *Journal of School Psychology*, 39(1), 45-69.

Buckner, J., Bassuk, E., Weinreb, L., and Brooks, M. (1999) Homelessness and its relation to the mental health and behavior of low-income school-age children. *Developmental Psychology*, 35(1), 246-257.

Burke-Harris, N. (2018). *The Deepest Well: Healing the Long-Term Effects of Childhood Adversity*. Boston, MA: Mariner Books.

California Research Bureau. (2007). *The Educational Success of Homeless Youth in California: Challenges and Solutions*. California Agencies, Paper 314.

Canfield, J. (2015). *School-based practice with children and youth experiencing homelessness*. New York, NY: Oxford University Press.

Canfield, J., & Teasley, M. (2015). The McKinney–Vento Homeless Assistance Act: School-based Practitioners' Place in Shaping the Policy's Future. *Children & Schools*, 37(2), 67-70.

Centers for Disease Control and Prevention. (2021). *Safely Distributing School Meals During Covid-19*. https://www.cdc.gov/coronavirus/2019-ncov/community/schools-childcare/safely-distributing-meals.html

Centers for Disease Control and Prevention. (2019). *Adverse childhood experiences*. www.cdc.gov/violenceprevention/childabuseandneglect/acestudy/index.html

Chatterjee, A., So, M., Dunleavy, S., & Oken, E. (2017). Quality health care for homeless families: Achieving the AAP recommendations for care of homeless children and youth. *Journal of Health Care for the Poor and Underserved*, 28(4), 1376.

Cherng, H., & Halpin, P. (2016). The importance of minority teachers: Student perceptions of minority versus White teachers. *Educational Researcher*, 45(7), 407-420.

Child Trends Data Bank (2015). *Homeless Children and Youth: Indicators on Children and Youth*. http://www.childtrends.org/?indicators=homeless-children-and-youth

Cohen, S., Glass, D., and Singer, J. (1973) Apartment noise, auditory discrimination, and reading ability in children, *Journal of Experimental Social Psychology*, 9, 407–422.

Collie, R. J., Shapka, J. D., & Perry, N. E. (2012). School climate and social–emotional learning: Predicting teacher stress, job satisfaction, and teaching efficacy. *Journal of Educational Psychology*, 104(4), 1189–1204.

Collins, S. (2013). From homeless teen to chronically homeless adult: A qualitative study of the impact of childhood events on adult homelessness. *Critical Social Work*, 14(2), 61-81.

Cornwall, G. (2018). *Is strength-based learning a magic bullet?* Hechinger Report. https://hechingerreport.org/strength-based-learning-magic-bullet/

Cueto, S. (2001) Breakfast and performance. (2001) *Public Health Nutrition*, 4(6A), 1429-1431.

Curtis, M, Corman, H., Noonan, K., & Reichman, N. (2014). Maternal depression as a risk factor for family homelessness. *American Journal of Public Health*, 104(9), 1664–1670.

Dank, M., Yahner, J., Madden, K., Bañuelos, I., Yu, L., Ritchie, A., Mora, M., & Conner, B. M. (2015). *Surviving the streets of New York: Experiences of LGBTQ youth, YMSM, and YWSW engaged in survival sex*. Washington, DC: The Urban Institute.

Dawson, C. (2018, December 4). *When students were bullied because of dirty clothes, a principal installed a free laundromat at school*. CNN.

De Las Nueces, D. (2016). Stigma and prejudice against individuals experiencing homelessness. In: Parekh R., Childs E. (eds) *Stigma and Prejudice. Current Clinical Psychiatry*. Humana Press.

Delmore, P. (2004) The door's open: Educating students who are homeless. *Principal Leadership*, 5(4), 32-36.

Desmond, M. (2017). *Evicted: Poverty and Profit in the American City*. New York, NY: Broadway Books.

Desautels, L. (2016). *"7 Ways to Calm a Young Brain in Trauma."* George Lucas Educational Foundation. https://www.edutopia.org/article/7-ways-calm-young-brain-trauma-lori-desautels

Dettlaff, A. J. (2015). *Racial Disproportionality and Disparities in the Child Welfare System*. Springer International Publishing AG.

Directors of Health Promotion and Education. (2005). *School Employee Wellness: A Guide for Protecting the Assets of Our Nation's Schools*. Washington, DC: Author. https://webnew.ped.state.nm.us/wp-content/uploads/2020/08/SHSB_School-Employee-Wellness.pdf

Diyaolu, M., Ye, C., Wild, H., Tennakoon, L., Spain, D., & Chao, S. (2021). Black children are disproportionately identified as victims of child abuse: A National Trauma Data Bank study. *Pediatrics*, 147.

D'Sa, S., Foley, D., Hannon, J., Strashun, S., Murphy, A., and O'Gorman, C. (2020). The psychological impact of childhood homelessness—a literature review. *Irish Journal of Medical Science*.

Duffield, B., Heybach, L., & Julianelle, P. (2007). *Educating children without housing: A primer on legal requirements and implementation strategies for educators, advocates and policymakers*. American Bar Association Commission on Homelessness and Poverty.

Duffield, B., & Lovell, P. (2008). *The economic crisis hits home: The unfolding increase in child and youth homelessness*. National Association for the Education of Homeless Children and Youth. Washington, DC.

Durlak, J., Weissberg, R., Dymnicki, A., Taylor, R., and Shellinger, K. (2011). The impact of enhancing students' social and emotional learning: A meta-analysis of school-based universal interventions. *Child Development*, 82(1), 405-432.

Duvall, D. and Vincent, N. (2009). Affect regulation of homeless youth once in the child welfare system. *Child and Adolescent Social Work*, 26, 155-173.

Dworsky, A. (2008). *Educating homeless children in Chicago: A case study of children in the family regeneration program*. Chapin Hall at the University of Chicago.

Eddowes, A. (1993) Education of younger homeless children in urban settings. *Education and Urban Society*, 25, 381-393.

Edwards, T. and Marshall, C. (2016). Undressing policy: a critical analysis of North Carolina (USA) public school dress codes. *Gender & Education*, 32, 732-750.

Emerson, J., & Lovitt, T. (2003). The educational plight of foster children in schools and what can be done about it. *Remedial and Special Education*. 24(4), 199-203.

Evans, G. W., Eckenrode, J., & Marcynyszynm L. A. (2010). Chaos and the macrosetting: The role of poverty and socioeconomic status. In G. W. Evans & T.D. Wachs (Eds.). *Chaos and its influence on children's development: An ecological perspective* (pp. 225-238). Washington, DC: American Psychological Association.

Evans, G. and Schamberg, M. (2009). Childhood poverty, chronic stress, and adult working memory. *Proceedings of the National Academy of Sciences*, 106(16), 6545-6549.

Endres, C. and Cicade, M. (2015). *Federal Data Summary, School Years 2011-2012 to 2013-2014: Education for homeless Children and Youth*. Greensboro, NC: National Center for Homeless Education.

Estola, E. (2003). Hope as work: Student teachers constructing their narrative identities. *Scandinavian Journal of Educational Research*, 47(2), 181-203.

Fantuzzo, J., LeBoeuf, W., Chen, C., Rouse, H., & Culhane, D. (2012). The unique and combined effects of homelessness and school mobility on the educational outcomes of young children. *Educational Researcher*, 41(9), 393-402.

Family and Youth Services Bureau. (2016). *Domestic Violence and Homelessness: Statistics*. https://www.acf.hhs.gov/fysb/resource/dv-homelessness-stats-2016

Federal Student Aid. (2020). *Dependency Status*. https://studentaid.gov/apply-for-aid/fafsa/filling-out/dependency

Federal Student Aid. (2021). Federal Student Aid and Homeless Youth. https://studentaid.gov/sites/default/files/homeless-youth.pdf

Federal Student Aid. (2019). *2019–20 Completing the FAFSA® Form*. https://studentaid.gov/sites/default/files/2019-20-completing-fafsa.pdf

Felitti, V., Anda, R., Nordenberg, D., Williamson, D., Spitz, A., Edwards, V., & Marks, J. (1998). Relationship of childhood abuse and household dysfunction to many of the leading causes of death in adults: The Adverse Childhood Experiences (ACE) Study. *American Journal of Preventive Medicine*, 14(4), 245-258.

Fernandes-Alcantara, A.L (2019). *Runaway and Homeless Youth: Demographics and Programs*. Congressional Research Service https://crsreports.congress.gov RL33785

Fiarman, S. and Benson, T. (2019). *Unconscious Bias in Schools: A Developmental Approach to Exploring Race and Racism*. Harvard Education Press.

Figley, C. R. (Ed.). (1995). *Compassion fatigue: Coping with secondary traumatic stress disorder in those who treat the traumatized* (No. 23). Psychology Press.

Friedman, K. (2019). *Three Ways to Build College Knowledge in High School. The Institute of Education Science Regional Educational Laboratory Program*. https://ies.ed.gov/ncee/edlabs/regions/appalachia/blogs/blog18_3-ways-to-build-college-knowledge-in-HS.asp#.

Fryer, R., Pager, D., and Spenkuch, J. (2013). Racial disparities in job finding and offered wages. *Journal of Law and Economics*, 56, 633-689.

Funkhouser, J., Riley, D., Suh, H. J., & Lennon, J. (2002). *The Education for Homeless Children And Youth Program: Learning To Succeed, Volume II: Educating Homeless Children And Youth: A Resource Guide To Promoting Practices*. United States Department of Education, Washington, D.C.

Gaffney, C. (2019). *When schools cause trauma. Learning for Justice*, 62, np.

Gargiulo, R. (2006). Homeless and disabled: Rights, responsibilities, and recommendations for serving young children with special needs. *Early Childhood Education Journal*, 33(5), 357-362.

Gershenson, S., Hart, C., Hyman, J., Lindsay, C., & Papageorge, N. (2018). *The long-run impacts of same-race teachers* (No. w25254). National Bureau of Economic Research.

Gewirtz, A., & Edleson, J. (2007). Young children's exposure to adult domestic violence: Towards a developmental risk and resilience framework for research and intervention. *Journal of Family Violence*, 22(3), 151-163.

Gewirtz, A., Hart-Shegos, E., & Medhanie, A. (2008). Psychosocial status of homeless children and youth in family supportive housing. *American Behavioral Scientist*, 51, 810 – 823.

Gewirtzman, R., & Fodor, I. (1987). The homeless child at school: From welfare hotel to classroom. *Child Welfare*, 66(3), 237-245.

Goldrick-Rab., S, Baker-Smith, C., Coca, V., Looker, E., and Williams, T. (2019). *College and University Basic Needs Insecurity: A National #RealCollege Survey Report*.

Gonzalez, M. (1990) School + Home = A Program for Educating Homeless Students. *Phi Delta Kappan,* 71(10), 785-787

Gordon, N. (2003) Iron deficiency and the intellect. *Brain and Development,* 25(1). 3-8.

Government Accountability Office. (2014). *Education of Homeless Students: Improved Program Oversight Needed.* Washington, DC: Author.

Gray L, & Taie S (2015). *Public School Teacher Attrition and Mobility in the First Five Years: Results from the First through Fifth Waves of the 2007-08 Beginning Teacher Longitudinal Study (NCES 2015-337).* U.S. Department of Education; Washington, DC: National Center for Education Statistics.

Grant, R., Bowen, S., McLean, D.E., Berman, D., Redlener, K., Redlener, I. (2007a). Asthma among homeless children in New York City: an update. *American Journal of Public Health,* 97(3), 448-450.

Grant, R., Shapiro, A., Joseph, S., Goldsmith, S., Rigual-Lynch, L., Redlener, I. (2007b). The health of homeless children revisited. *Advances in Pediatrics,* 54, 173-87.

Greene, B. (2010). *Hunger grows in the heartland.* CNN.http://www.cnn.com/2010/OPINION/11/14/greene. hunger.backpacks/index.html?hpt=C2

Gregory, A., and Weinstein, R. (2008). The discipline gap and African Americans: Defiance or cooperation in the high school classroom. *Journal of School Psychology,* 46, 455–475.

Gultekin, L., Brush, B., Ginier, E., Cordom, A., and Dowdell, E. (2020). Health risks and outcomes of homelessness in school-age children and youth: A scoping review of the literature. *The Journal of School Nursing,* 36(1), 10-18.

Hallett, R. and Skrla, L. (2017). *Serving Students Who Are Homeless.* New York, NY: Teachers College Press.

Harpaz-Rotem, I., Rosenheck, R., and Desai, R. (2006) Mental health of children exposed to maternal mental illness and homelessness. *Community Mental Health Journal,* 42(5), 437-448.

Hart-Shegos, E. (1999). *Homelessness and its effects on children.* Minneapolis, MN: Family Housing Fund.

Havlik, S., Sanders, C., and Wilson, E. (2018). Preparing students experiencing homelessness for College: Considerations for counselors and other supportive personnel. *Journal of College Access,* 4(1), 5-19.

Hayes, M., Zonneville, M., & Bassuk, E. (2013). *The SHIFT Study final report: Service and housing interventions for families in transition.* Newton, MA: National Center on Family Homelessness.

Heinlein, L., & Shinn, M. (2000) School mobility and student achievement in an urban setting. *Psychology in the Schools,* 37(4), 349-357.

Henry, M., Watt, R., Rosenthal, L., and Shivji, A. (2017). *The 2017 Annual Homeless Assessment Report to Congress.* https://files.hudexchange.info/resources/documents/2017-AHAR-Part-1.pdf

Herbers, J., Cutuli, J., Monn, A., Narayan, A., & Masten, A. (2014). Trauma, adversity, and parent–child relationships among young children experiencing homelessness. *Journal of abnormal child psychology,* 42(7), 1167-1174.

Hernandez Jozefowicz-Simbeni, D. and Israel, N. (2006). Services to homeless students and families: The McKinney-Vento Act and its implications for school social work practice. *Children & Schools,* 28(1), 37-44.

Herth, K. (1998). Hope as seen through the eyes of homeless children. *Journal of Advanced Nursing,* 28(5), 1053-1062.

Hill, A. (2011). *The cost of caring: An investigation in the effects of teaching traumatized children in urban elementary settings.* Open Access Dissertations. 388. https://schol- arworks.umass.edu/open_access_ dissertations/388

Hope Center for College, *Community, and Justice at Temple University.* (2020). 2019 #realcollege Survey School Report. Philadelphia, PA: Author.

Hope Center for College, Community, and Justice at Temple University. (2020). *#RealCollege 2021: Basic Needs Insecurity During the Ongoing Pandemic.* Philadelphia, PA: Author.

Hope, E., Skoog, A., and Jagers, R. (2014). "It'll never be the white kids, it'll always be us": Black high school students' evolving critical analysis of racial discrimination and inequality in schools. *Journal of Adolescent Research,* 30, 83-112.

Horowitz, S., Springer, C., & Kose, G. (1988). Stress in hotel children: The effects of homelessness on attitudes toward school. *Children's Environments Quarterly,* 5(1), p. 34-36.

Hudson, A., Nyamathi, A., Greengold, B., Slagle, A., Koniak-Griffin, D., Khalilifard, F., and Getzoff, D. (2010). Health-seeking challenges among homeless youth. *Nursing Research* 59(3), 212-218.

Hupe, T., & Stevenson, M. (2019). Teachers' intentions to report suspected child abuse: The influence of compassion fatigue. *Journal of Child Custody,* 16(4), 364-386.

Hydon, S., Wong, M., Langley, A., Stein, B., and Kataoka, S. (2015). Hydon, S., (2015). Preventing secondary traumatic stress in educators. *Child and Adolescent Psychiatric Clinics,* 24(2), 319-333.

Ingram, E., Bridgeland, J., Reed, B., and Atwell, M. (2016). *Hidden in Plain Sight: Homeless Students in*

References

America's Public Schools. Washington, DC: Civic Enterprises.

Institute for Child Poverty and Homelessness. (2016). *Aftershocks: The lasting impact of homelessness on student achievement.* New York, NY: Author.

Institute for Children, Poverty, & Homelessness. (2017). T*aken Away: The Prevalence of Homeless Children in Foster Care.* New York, NY: Author. https://www.icphusa.org/reports/taken-away-2/

Jahiel, R. (1987). The situation of homelessness. In Bingham, R., Green, R., & White, S. (Eds.), *The homeless in contemporary society* (p. 99-118). Newbury Park, CA: Sage Publications, Inc.

James, B., & Lopez, P. (2003). Transporting homeless students to increase stability: A case study of two Texas districts. *Journal of Negro Education, 72*(1), 126-140.

Jaycox L., Langley A., and Dean K. (2009). *Support for Students Exposed to Trauma: The SSET Program— Lesson Plans, Worksheets, and Materials.* Santa Monica: RAND Corporation. http://www.rand.org/pubs/ technical_reports/TR675.html

Jelleyman, T., & Spencer, N. (2008). Residential mobility in childhood and health outcomes: A systematic review. *Journal of Epidemiology and Community Health, 62*(7), 584-592.

Jennings, P. (2018). *The Trauma-Sensitive Classroom: Building Resilience with Compassionate Teaching.* W.W. Norton & Company.

Johnson, J., Jr. (1992). Educational support services for homeless children and youth. In J. H. Stronge (Ed.), *Educating homeless children and adolescents: Evaluating policy and practice* (pp. 153-176). Newbury Park, CA: Sage Publications, Inc.

Johnson, R., Rew, L., and Sternglanz, R. (2006). The relationship between childhood sexual abuse and sexual health practices of homeless adolescents. *Adolescence,* 41, 221-234.

Jozefowicz-Simbeni, D. M. H., & Israel, N. (2006). Services to homeless students and families: The McKinney-Vento Act and its implications for school social work practice. *Children & Schools,* 28(1), 37-44

Julianelle, P. (2007). *The educational successes of homeless youth in California: Challenges and solutions.* California Research Bureau. http://www.library.ca.gov/crb/CRBSearch.aspx

Karabanow, J. (2004). *Being young and homeless: Understanding how youth enter and exit street life.* New York: Peter Lang Publishing, Inc.

Keagy, K. (2020). "*South Floyd Elementary receives donation from Whirlpool to begin laundry program.*" WSAZ NewsChannel 3. https://www.wsaz.com/2020/09/18/south-floyd-elementary-receives-donation-from-whirlpool-to-begin-laundry-program/

Kelly, M. (2013). P*oor concentration: Poverty reduces brainpower needed for navigating other areas of life.* Princeton University Office of Communications.

Kenny, M. C. (2001). Child abuse reporting: Teachers' perceived deterrents. Child Abuse & Neglect, 25(1), 81–92.

Khoo, E., Hyvonen, U., and Nygren, L. (2002). Child welfare or child protection: Uncovering Swedish and Canadian orientations to social intervention in child maltreatment. *Qualitative Social Work,* 1 (4), 451-471.

Kidd, S. A., & Davidson, L. (2007). "You have to adapt because you have no other choice": The stories of strength and resilience of 208 homeless youth in New York City and Toronto. *Journal of Community Psychology,* 35(2), 219-238.

Koball, H. and Jiang, Y. (2018). *Basic facts about low-income children: Children under 18 years, 2016.* New York: National Center for Children in Poverty, Columbia University Mailman School of Public Health.

Kiesler, C. (1991). Homelessness and public policy priorities. *American Psychologist, 46*(11), 1245-1252.

Kim, J. (2013). Confronting invisibility: Early childhood pre-service teachers' beliefs toward homeless children. *Early Childhood Education Journal,* 41, 161-169.

Kliman, J. (1968) *Psychological emergencies of childhood.* New York: Grune and Stratton.

Koegel P, Melamid E, and Burnam A. (1995). Childhood risk factors for homelessness among homeless adults. *American Journal of Public Health,* 85(12), 1642–1649.

Korinek, L., Walther-Thomas, C., & Laycock, V. (1992). Educating special needs homeless children and youth. In J. H. Stronge (Ed.), *Educating Homeless Children and Adolescents: Evaluating Policy and Practice* (pp. 133-152). Newbury Park, CA: Sage Publications, Inc.

Lacoe, J. (2013). *Too scared to learn? The academic consequences of feeling unsafe at school.* Working Paper #02–13. Institute for Education and Social Policy. https://eric.ed.gov/?id=ED556783

Lander, J. (2018). *Helping teachers manage the weight of trauma. Perspectives + Opinions.* Cambridge, MA: Harvard Graduate School of Education. https://www.gse.harvard.edu/news/uk/18/09/helping-teachers-manage-weight-trauma

Learning for Justice. (2015). "I thought about quitting today." *Learning for Justice Magazine,* 51. https://www.learningforjustice.org/magazine/fall-2015/toolkit-for-i-thought-about-quitting-today

Lever, N., Mathis, E., and Mayworm, A. (2017). School mental health is not just for students: Why teacher and school staff wellness matters. *Report on Emotional & Behavioral Disorders in Youth,* 17(1), 6.

94

Lippert, A., and Lee, B. (2020). *Adult and child food insecurity among homeless and precariously-housed families at the close of the twentieth century*. Population Research and Policy Review.

Loewenstein, G. (1996). Out of control: Visceral influences on behavior. *Organizational Behavior and Human Decision Processes*, 65, 272-292.

Love, B. (2020). *We want to do more than survive: Abolitionist teaching and the pursuit of educational freedom*. Boston, MA: Beacon Press.

Lubell, J. and Brennan, M. (2007). *Framing the issues – the positive impacts of affordable housing on education*. Washington, DC: Center for Housing Policy.

Lubell, J., Crain, R., and Cohen, R. (2007). *Framing the issues – the positive impacts of affordable housing on health*. Washington, DC: Center for Housing Policy.

Lupien, A., Fiocco, A., Wan, N., Maheu, F., Lord, C., Schramek, T., and Tu, M. (2005). Stress hormones and human memory function across the lifespan. *Psychoneuroendocrinology*, 30, p. 225-242.

Lynch W. (1965). *Images of Hope: Imagination as Healer of Hopeless*. Baltimore, Maryland: Helicon.

Mani, A., Mullainathan, S., Shafir, E., and Zhao, J. (2013). Poverty impedes cognitive function. *Science*, 314, 976-980.

Manna, R. (2009). *130 FAQs and practical answers from Scholastic's teacher helpline*. New York, NY: Scholastic.

Marcal, K. (2017). A theory of mental health and optimal service delivery for homeless children. *Child and Adolescent Social Work Journal*, 34, 349-359.

Marshall, A. T., Betts, S., Kan, E. C., McConnell, R., Lanphear, B. P., & Sowell, E. R. (2020). Association of lead-exposure risk and family income with childhood brain outcomes. *Nature medicine*, 26(1), 91-97.

Maslow, A. (1954). *Motivation and personality*. Harpers.

Masten, A., Best, K., and Garmezy, N. (1990). Resilience and development: Contributions from the study of children who overcome adversity. *Development and Psychopathology*, 2(4), 425-444.

Masten, A., Fiat, A, Labella, M., & Strack, R. (2015). Educating homeless and highly mobile students: Implications of research on risk and resilience. *School Psychology Review*, 44(3), 315-330.

Masten, A., Miliotis, D., Graham-Bermann, S. A., Ramirez, M., & Neemann, J. (1993). Children in homeless families: Risks to mental health and development. *Journal of Consulting and Clinical Psychology*, 61(2), 335-343.

Masten, A. and Sesma, A. (1999) *Risk and resilience among children homeless in Minneapolis*. Center for Urban and Regional Affairs, 29(1), 1-6.

Masten, A., Sesma, A., Si-Asar, R., Lawrence, C., Miliotis, D., Dionne, J. (1997). Educational risks for children experiencing homelessness. *Journal of School Psychology*, 35, 27-46.

Matias, C. and Liou, D. (2015). Tending to the heart of communities of color: Toward critical race teacher activism. *Urban Education*, 50, 601-625.

Mawhinney-Rhoads, L., & Stahler, G. (2006). Educational policy and reform for homeless students: An overview. *Education and Urban Society*, 38(3), 288-306.

Mayo Clinic. (2021). *Job Burnout: How to Spot it and Take Action*. https://www.mayoclinic.org/healthy-lifestyle/adult-health/in-depth/burnout/art-20046642

Maza, J. A., & Hall, P. L. (1990). No fixed address: The effects of homelessness on families and children. *Child and Youth Services*, 14(1), 35–47.

McKinney-Vento *Homeless Assistance Act. 42 U.S. Code § 11302*.

McKinney-Vento *Homeless Assistance Act. 42 U.S. Code § 11434a*.

McLoyd, VC (1998) Socioeconomic disadvantage and child development. *American Psychology*, 53(2), 185-204

Medcalf, N. (2008). *Kidwatching in Josie's world*. Lanham, MD: University Press of America, Inc.

Mihaly, L. (1991, January). *Homeless families: Failed policies and young victims*.Washington, DC: Children's Defense Fund.

Miller, P., Pavlakis, A., Samartino, L. and Bourgeois, A. (2015). Brokering educational opportunity for homeless students and their families. *International Journal of Qualitative Studies in Education*, 28(6), 730-749.

Milner, H.R. (2010). *Start Where You Are, But Don't Stay There*. Cambridge, MA: Harvard Education Press.

Minahan, J. (2019). Trauma-informed teaching strategies. *Educational Leadership*, 77(2), 30-35.

Minahan, J., & Rappaport, N. (2012). *The behavior code: A practical guide to understanding and teaching the most challenging students*. Cambridge, MA: Harvard Education Press.

Molnar, J., Rath, W., and Klein, T. (1990). Constantly compromised: The impact of homelessness on children. *Journal of Social Issues*, 46(4), 109-124.

Moore, J. (2013). *Teaching and Classroom Strategies for Homeless and Highly Mobile Students*. Greensboro, NC: National Center for Homeless Education.

Morris, R. and Butt, R. (2003). Parents' perspectives on homelessness and its effects on the educational development of their children. *Journal of School Nursing*, 19, 43-50.

References

Morton, M., Dworsky, A., & Curry, S. (2017). National prevalence study of youth homelessness: VoYC component report to the U.S. Department of Housing and Urban Development. Chicago, IL: Chapin Hall.

Murphy, J. and Tobin, K. (2011). *Homelessness Comes to School.* Corwin Press.

Myers, M., & Popp, P. (2003). *Unlocking potential! What educators need to know about homelessness and special education.* http://www.wm.edu/hope/infobrief/personnel-complete.pdf

Mykyta, L., & Macartney, S. (2011). *The effects of recession on household composition: 'doubling up' and economic well-being.* US Census Bureau. Social, Economic and Household Statistics Division Working Paper, 4.

National Association for the Education of Homeless Children and Youth (2010). *A critical moment: Child and youth homelessness in our nation's schools.* Retrieved October 2, 2010 from http://www.naehcy.org/criticalmoment.htm

National Black Child Development Association. (1989) *Who will care when parents can't? A study of black children in foster care.* Washington, DC: Author.

National Center for Education Statistics. (2020a). *Concentration of Public School Students Eligible for Free or Reduced-Price Lunch.* https://nces.ed.gov/programs/coe/indicator_clb.asp

National Center for Education Statistics. (2020b). *Racial/Ethnic Enrollment in Public Schools.* https://nces.ed.gov/programs/coe/indicator_cge.asp

National Center for Homeless Education. (2017). I*dentifying Children and Youth in Homeless Situations.* Greensboro, NC: Author.

National Center for Homeless Education. (2020). *Federal Data Summary, School Years 2015-16 to 2017-18. Education for Homeless Children and Youth.* Greensboro, NC: Author.

National Center for Homeless Education. (2006). *Housing agency and school district collaborations to serve homeless and highly mobile students.* Greensboro, NC: Author.

National Center for Homeless Education. (2017). *Identifying Children and Youth in Homeless Situations.* Greensboro, NC: Author.

National Center on Family Homelessness. (2009). *America's youngest outcasts: State report card on child homelessness.* Newton, MA: Author.

National Center on Safe and Supportive Learning Environments. (2021). *Secondary Traumatic Stress.* https://safesupportivelearning.ed.gov/resources/secondary-traumatic-stress

National Child Traumatic Stress Network. (2017). *SSET: Support for Students Exposed to Trauma: School Support for Childhood Trauma.* http://traumaawareschools.org/resources-materials/3162/SSET_General_012417.pdf?1485787289

National Child Traumatic Stress Network. (2003). *What is child traumatic stress?* https://www.samhsa.gov/sites/default/files/programs_campaigns/childrens_mental_health/what-is-child-traumatic-stress.pdf

National Coalition for the Homeless (2021). *Types of Homelessness.* Washington, DC: Author. http://nationalhomeless.org/about-homelessness/

National Coalition for the Homeless. (1987) *Broken lives: Denial of education to homeless children.* Washington, DC: Author.

National Coalition for the Homeless. (2006) *McKinney Vento Act: NCH Fact Sheet #18.* Retrieved November 16, 2010 from http://www.nationalhomeless.org/publications/facts/McKinne.pdf

National Council of State Legislatures. (2019). *Youth Homelessness Overview.* https://www.ncsl.org/research/human-services/homeless-and-runaway-youth.aspx

National Research Council. (2013). *Confronting commercial sexual exploitation and sex trafficking of minors in the United States.* National Academies Press.

Neiman, L. (1988). A critical review of resiliency literature and its relevance to homeless children. *Children's Environments Quarterly,* 5(1), 1-25.

Newman, R., & Beck, L. (1996). Educating homeless children: One experiment in collaboration. In J. Cibulka and W. Kritek (Eds.). *Coordination among schools, families, and communities: Prospects for educational reform* (pp. 95-133). Albany: State University of New York Press.

New Jersey Office of the Child Advocate. (2008). *Protecting Children: A Review of Investigations of Institutional Child Abuse and Neglect.* Trenton, NJ: Author.

Noble, K.G., McCandliss, B.D., Farah, M. (2007). Socioeconomic gradients predict individual differences in neurocognitive abilities. *Developmental Science,* 10, p. 464–480.

Noddings, N. (1993). Excellence as a guide to educational conversation. *Teachers College Record,* 94, 730-730.

Nolan, J., Cole, T., Wroughton, J., Riffe, H., & Clayton-Code, K. (2013). Assessment of risk factors for truancy of children in grades K-12 using survival analysis. *Journal of At-Risk Issues,* 17 (2), 23-30.

Noll, E. and Watkins, R. (2003). The impact of homelessness on children's literary experiences. *The reading teacher*, 57(4), 362-372.

Nuñez, R. (1994a). Access to success: Meeting the educational needs of homeless children and families. *Social Work in Education*, 16(1), 21-30.

Nuñez, R. (1994b). *Hopes, dreams, and promise*. New York: Institute for Children and Poverty.

Nuñez, R. and Collignon, K. (1997). Creating a community of learning for homeless children. *Educational Leadership*, 55(2), 56-60.

Oberle, E., & Schonert-Reichl, K. (2016). Stress contagion in the classroom? The link between classroom teacher burnout and morning cortisol in elementary school students. *Social Science & Medicine*, 159, 30-37.

Obradovic, J., Long, J., Cutuli, J., Chan, C., Hinz, E., Heistad, D., & Masten, A. (2009). Academic achievement of homeless and highly mobile children in an urban school district: Longitudinal evidence on risk, growth, and resilience. *Development and psychopathology*, 21(2), 493.

OECD. (2014). *TALIS 2013 results: An international perspective on teaching and learning*, TALIS. Paris, France: OECD Publishing.

Okonofua, J. and Eberhardt, J. (2015). Two strikes: Race and the disciplining of young students. *Psycholgical Science*, 26(5), 617–624.

Olson, C. (1999). Nutrition and health outcomes associated with food insecurity and hunger. *Journal of Nutrition*, 129(2S). 521-524.

Parpouchi, M., Moniruzzaman, A., & Somers, J. M. (2021). The association between experiencing homelessness in childhood or youth and adult housing stability in Housing First. *BMC Psychiatry*, 21(1), 1-14.

Patrick, R. (2020, February 11). *State, Riverview Gardens settle suit of education for homeless students. St. Louis Post Dispatch*. https://www.stltoday.com/news/local/crime-and-courts/state-riverview-gardens-settle-suit-over-education-for-homeless-students/article_eb11cb47-91ca-5681-9784-6648ab89557f.html

Pavlakis, A. (2015). Reaching all families: Family, school, and community partnerships amid homelessness and high mobility in an urban district. *Urban Education*, 46, 445-475.

Pennsylvania Legal Aid. (2010). *Lawsuit boosts school access for homeless students in Pennsylvania*. http://www.palegalaid.net/news/palawhelporg-news/lawsuit-boosts-school-access- homeless-students-pennsylvania

Penuel, W., & Davey, T. (1998). *Meta-analysis of McKinney programs in Tennessee*. Paper presented at the Annual Meeting of the American Educational Research Association, San Diego, CA, April 13-17, 1998.

Percy M. (1995) Children from homeless families describe what is special in their lives. *Holistic Nursing Practice* 9(4), 24-33.

Perlman, L., and Saakvitne, K. (1995). *Trauma and the Therapist*. Norton.

Perna, L. (2006). Studying college access and choice: A proposed conceptual model. In J. C. Smart (Ed.), *Higher Education: Handbook of theory and research*, (pp. 99–157). Routledge.

Piccolo, L. and Noble, K. (2018). Perceived stress is associated with smaller hippocampal volume in adolescence: Perceived stress effects in adolescent brain. *Psychophysiology*, 55(5), e13025.

Pohlack, S., Meyer, P., Cacciaglia, R., Liebscher, C., Ridder, S., and Flor, H. (2014). Bigger is better! Hippocampal volume and declarative memory performance in healthy young men. *Brain Structure and Function*, 219(1), 255-267.

Portwood, S., Shears, J., Nelson, E., & Thomas, M. (2015). Examining the impact of family services on homeless children. *Child & Family Social Work*, 20(4), 480-493.

Powers, J., & Jaklitsch, B. (1993). Reaching the hard to reach: Educating homeless adolescents in urban settings. *Education and Urban Society*, 24(4), 394-409.

Powers-Costello, B., & Swick, K. (2011). Transforming teacher constructs of children and families who are homeless. *Early Childhood Education Journal*, 39(3), 207-212.

Project Implicit. (2021). https://implicit.harvard.edu/implicit/

Quint, S. (1994). *Schooling homeless children: A working model for America's public schools*. New York: Teachers College Press.

Rafferty, Y. (1990) *The challenge of educating children who are homeless*. Paper presented at the Annual Meeting of the American Public Health Association, October 3, 1990.

Rafferty, Y. and Rollins, N. (1989) *Learning in limbo: The educational deprivation of homeless children*. Long Island City, NY: Advocates for Children of New York, Inc.

Rafferty, Y., and Shinn, M. (1991). The impact of homelessness on children. *American Psychologist*, 46(11), 1170-1179.

Rafferty, Y., Shinn, M., & Weitzman, B. C. (2004). Academic achievement among formerly homeless adolescents and their continuously housed peers. *Journal of School Psychology*, 42, 179-199.

Rawana, E.P., Brownlee, K., Whitley, J. Rawana, J., Franks, J., and Walker, D. (2009). *Strengths in Motion: A Strengths-Based Approach to Enhance Positive School Climate and Address Issues of Bullying and School*

References

Violence. Thunder Bay, ON: Centre of Excellence for Children and Adolescents with Special Needs.

Reed-Victor, E., Popp, P., & Myers, M. (2003). *Using the best that we know: Supporting young children experiencing homelessness.* Virginia Department of Education: Project HOPE-Virginia.

Rescorla, L., Parker, R., & Stolley, P. (1991). Ability, achievement, and adjustment in homeless children. *American Journal of Orthopsychiatry*, 61(2), 210-220.

Rew, L., Whittaker, T., Taylor-Seehafer, M., & Smith, L. (2005). Sexual health risks and protective resources in gay, lesbian, bisexual, and heterosexual homeless youth. *Journal for Specialists in Pediatric Nursing*, 10(1), 11-19.

Riddle, T. and Sinclair, S. (2019). *Racial disparities in school-based disciplinary actions are associated with county-level rates of racial bias.* Proceedings of the National Academy of Sciences, 116 (17), 8255-8260.

Robinson, K. and Harris, A. (2014). *The broken compass: Parental involvement with children's education.* Harvard University Press.

Rouse, H., & Fantuzzo, J. (2009). Multiple risks and educational well-being: A population-based investigation of threats to early school success. *Early Childhood Research Quarterly*, 24(1). 1-14.

Rubin, D., Erickson, C., San Augstin, M., Clearly, S., Allen, K., and Cohen, P. (1996) Cognitive and academic functioning of homeless children compared with housed children. *Pediatrics*, 97(3), 289-295.

Sakai-Bizmark, R., Chang, R., Mena, L., Webber, E., Marr, E., & Kwong, K. (2019). Asthma hospitalizations among homeless children in New York state. *Pediatrics*, 144(2).

Saleebey, D. (2008). *Commentary on the strengths perspective in social work practice (2nd Ed).* Toronto, Canada: Pearson Education.

Salmivalli, C., & Voeten, M. (2004). Connections between attitudes, group norms, and behaviour in bullying situations. *International Journal of Behavioral Development*, 28, 246 –258.

Samuels, J., Shinn, M., and Buckner, J. (2010). *Homeless Children: Update on Research, Policy, Programs, and Opportunities.* Prepared for the Office of the Assistant Secretary for Planning and Evaluation, U.S. Department of Health and Human Services. Delmar, NY: Policy Research Associates, Inc.

Santos, M. (2017). *The Most Frequently Asked Questions on the Education Rights of Children and Youth in Homeless Situations.* Tucker, GA: National Association for the Education of Homeless Children and Youth.

Schmitz, C., Wagner, J., and Menke, E. (1995) Homelessness as one component of housing instability and its impact on the development of children in poverty. *Journal of Social Distress and the Homeless*, 4(4), 301-318.

SchoolHouse Connection. (2021). *Signs of Potential Homelessness in a Virtual Learning World.* https://schoolhouseconnection.org/wp-content/uploads/2020/08/signsofhomelessness-virtual.pdf

SchoolHouse Connection. (2012). *Tips for Teachers and Staff: How to Support Students Experiencing Homelessness.*https://schoolhouseconnection.org/tips-for-teachers-staff-how-to-support-students-experiencing-homelessness/

Scott C., et al. v Riverview Gardens (2018). *Case No. 18-4162, United States District Court, Western District of Missouri, Central Division.* Retrieved from http://www.publiccounsel.org/tools/assets/files/1054.pdf

Shane, P. (1996). *What about America's homeless children?* Thousand Oaks, CA: Sage Publications, Inc.

Shields, C., & Warke, A. (2010). The invisible crisis: Connecting schools with homeless families. *Journal of School Leadership*, 20(6), 789-819.

Shinn, M. (2009). *Ending Homelessness for Families: The Evidence for Affordable Housing.* Washington, DC: National Alliance to End Homelessness and Enterprise Community Partners.

Shinn, M., Schteingart, J., Williams, N., Carlin-Mathis, J., Bialo-Karagis, N., Becker-Klein, R., and Weitzman, B. (2008). Long-term associations of homelessness with children's wellbeing. *American Behavioral Scientist*, 51(6), 798-808.

Siegel, D. and Bryson, T.P. (2011). *The Whole-Brain Child.* New York, NY: Delacorte Press.

Simmons, R. (2003). *Odd Girl Out: The Hidden Culture of Aggression in Girls.* Orlando, FL: Harcourt Books.

Sinatra, R. (2007) Literacy success with homeless children. *The Journal of At-Risk Issues*, 13(2), 1-9.

Sizemore, C. (2016). Compassion fatigue: The silent thief in our schools. *The Working Lives of Educators*, 11(18), 1–4.

Smrekar, C. E., & Owens, D. E. (2003). "It's a way of life for us": High mobility and high achievement in Department of Defense schools. *Journal of Negro Education*, 165-177.

Snyder, C. (2005). *Measuring hope in children. In What do children need to flourish?* Springer: Boston, MA.

Silva, J., Langhout, R., Kohfeldt, D., and Gurrola, E. (2015). Good" and "bad" kids? A race and gender analysis of effective behavioral support in an elementary school. *Urban Education*, 50, 707-811.

Spears, J. (2017). *Flooded Desire: How Water Changes Perception.* Unpublished Teacher-Researcher Project, Louisiana State University.

Stauffer, R. (2021). *The Housing Crisis for Students Was Bad Before COVID — and It's Only Getting Worse.*

https://www.apartmenttherapy.com/college-student-housing-crisis-covid-36865268

Stevens, C., Tullis, R., Sanchez, K. and Gonzalez, J. (1991) *Description of the Lighted Schoolhouse Program (1990-1991)*. Houston: Houston Independent School District Department of Research and Evaluation.

Stronge, J. (2000). *Educating homeless children and youth: An introduction. In J.H. Stronge & E. Reed-Victor (Eds.), Educating homeless students: Promising practices* (pp. 1-19). Larchmont, NY: Eye on Education, Inc.

Stronge, J., & Hudson, K. (1999). Educating homeless children and youth with dignity and care. *Journal for a Just and Caring Education*, 5(1), 7-18.

Stronge, J. (1993). From access to success. *Journal of Education and Urban Society*, 25(4), 340- 360.

Suitts, S. (2016). Students facing poverty: The new majority. *Educational Leadership*, 74(3), 36-40.

Support for Students Exposed to Trauma. (2021). http://ssetprogram.org

Swearer, S., & Hymel, S. (2015). Understanding the psychology of bullying: Moving toward a social-ecological diathesis–stress model. *American Psychologist*, 70(4), 344.

Swick, K. (2009). Strengthening homeless parents with young children through meaningful parent education and support. *Early Childhood Education Journal*, 36(4), 327-332.

Swick, K. (2008). The dynamics of violence and homelessness among young families. *Early Childhood Education Journal*, 36(1), 81-85.

Swick, K. (2000). Building effective awareness programs for homeless students among staff, peers, and community members. In J.H. Stronge & E. Reed-Victor (Eds.), *Educating homeless students: Promising practices* (pp. 165-182). Larchmont, NY: Eye on Education, Inc.

Swick, K. (1996). Early childhood teachers reconstruct their views about homeless families. *Journal of Early Childhood Teacher Education*, 17(1), 26–36.

Swick, K., & Bailey, L. (2004). Communicating effectively with parents and families who are homeless. *Early Childhood Education Journal*, 32(3), 211-215.

Tacoma Community College. (2021). *College Housing Assistance Program (CHAP)*. https://www.tacomacc.edu/tcc-life/life-resources/college_housing_assistance_program

Taie, S., & Goldring, R. (2020). *Characteristics of Public and Private Elementary and Secondary School Teachers in the United States: Results from the 2017-18 National Teacher and Principal Survey. First Look. NCES 2020-142*. Washington, DC: National Center for Education Statistics.

The Road Map Project. (2015). *2013-2014 Regional Technical Report*. Seattle, WA: Community Center for Education Results.

Tierney, W. and Hallett, R. (2012). Social Capital and Homeless Youth: Influence of Residential Instability on College Access. *Metropolitan Universities Journal*, 22(3), 46-62.

Tierney, W., Gupton, J., & Hallett, R. (2008). *Transitions to adulthood for homeless adolescents: Education and public policy*. Center for Higher Education Policy Analysis (CHEPA).

Terrasi, S., & de Galarce, P. C. (2017). Trauma and learning in America's classrooms. *Phi Delta Kappan*, 98(6), 35–41.

Tobin, K. (2016). Homelessness and academic achievement: Evidence from a large urban area. *Urban Education*, 51(2), 197-220.

Tobin, K. (2015). *Expert report submitted to the Circuit Court of the Second Judicial Circuit in and for Leon County, State of Florida, as part of Citizen for Strong Schools v Florida State Board of Education. Case No. 09-CA-4534.*

Tobin, K. (2011). *Identifying best practices for homeless students*. Dissertation, Vanderbilt University. https://ir.vanderbilt.edu/handle/1803/13378

Tobin, K. and Murphy, J. (2012). A policy agenda for addressing homelessness. *School Leadership Review*, 7(1), 71-97.

Toshalis, E. (2015). *Make me! Understanding and engaging student resistance in school*. Cambridge, MA: Harvard Education Press.

Trivedi, S. (2019). The harm of child removal. *New York University Review of Law and Social Change*, 43, 525-580.

Turney, K. and Wildeman, C. (2017). Adverse childhood experiences among children place in and adopted from foster care: Evidence from a nationally representative survey. *Child Abuse and Neglect*, 64, 117-129.

United States Conference of Mayors. (1991) *A status report on hunger and homelessness in America's cities: 1990*. Washington, DC: Author.

Unite, B. (2019). *The Types of Homelessness*. https://artfromthestreets.org/blogs/news/the-types-of-homelessness

United States Department of Education Data Dashboard. (2021). *McKinney-Vento Facts*. https://eddataexpress.ed.gov/dashboard/homeless

United States Department of Housing and Urban Development. (2021). *Glossary of HUD Terms*. Washington,

References

DC: Office of Police Development and Research.

United States Department of Housing and Urban Development. (2020). *Homeless Emergency Assistance and Rapid Transition to Housing Act.* https://www.hudexchange.info/homelessness-assistance/hearth-act/

United States Department of Housing and Urban Development. (2010). *Federal definition of homeless.* http://portal.hud.gov/portal/page/portal/HUD/topics/homelessness/definition

Van Manen, M. (2000). Moral language and pedagogical experience. *The Journal of Curriculum Studies, 32*(2), 315-327.

Vespa, M. (2020). *"What's the difference between houseless and homeless?"* KGW8 News, August 13, 2020. https://www.kgw.com/article/news/local/homeless/whats-the-difference-homeless-houseless-street-roots-portland-oregon/283-76dc7044-d7fe-411f-bb23-b4097ac49686

Wade, R., Shea, J., Rubin, D., & Wood, J. (2014). Adverse childhood experiences of low-income urban youth. *Pediatrics, 134*(1), 13-20.

Waguespack, D., and Ryan, B. (2020). *State Index on Youth Homelessness.* True Colors United and the National Homelessness Law Center.

Walker, P. (2013). *Complex PTSD: From Surviving to Thriving.* Lafayette, CA: Azure Coyote Publishing.

Watson, N., Steffen, B., Martin, M., & Vandenbroucke, D. (2017). *Worst Case Housing Needs Report to Congress, 2017.* Washington, DC: US Department of Housing and Urban Development.

Weinreb, L., Wehler, C., Perloff, J., Scott, R., Hosmer, D., Sagor, L., & Gundersen, C. (2002). Hunger: Its impact on children's health and mental health. *Pediatrics,* 110.

Weisbuch, M., Pauker, K., & Ambady, N. (2009). The subtle transmission of race bias via televised nonverbal behavior. *Science, 326*(5960), 1711-1714.

Weinger, S. (1998). Children living in poverty: Their perceptions of career opportunities. *Families in Society: The Journal of Contemporary Human Services,* 79, 320-330.

Welcoming Schools. (2021). *What Can We Do? Bias, Bullies, and Bystanders.* Washington, DC: The Human Rights Campaign Foundation. https://www.welcomingschools.org/resources/our-films/what-can-we-do/

Weston, K., Anderson-Butcher, D., and Burke, R. (2008). Developing a comprehensive curriculum framework for teacher preparation in expanded school mental health. *Advances in School Mental Health Promotion, 1*(4), 25-41.

White, C., O'Brien, K., Pecora, P., Kessler, R., Sampson, N., and Hwang, I. (2012). *Texas Foster Care Alumni Study Technical Report: Executive Summary.* Casey Family Programs.

Whitman, B., Stretch, J., and Accardo, P. (1987). *Testimony presented before the U.S. House of Representatives Select Committee on Youth, Children, and Families. The crisis in homelessness: Effects on children and families,* 125. Washington, DC: U.S. Government Printing Office.

Will, M. (2020). *The success of social-emotional learning hinges on teachers.* Education Week, April 7, 2020. https://www.edweek.org/leadership/the-success-of-social-emotional-learning-hinges-on-teachers/2020/04

Willard, A. and Kulinna, P. (2012). Summer literacy interventions for homeless children living in transitional housing. *The Journal of At-Risk Issues,* 17, 15-22.

Williams, B., & Korinek, L. (2000). In J.H. Stronge & E. Reed-Victor (Eds.), *Educating homeless students: Promising practices* (pp. 183-201). Larchmont, NY: Eye on Education, Inc.

Wong, J., Elliott, L., Reed, S., Ross, W., McGuirk, P., & Tallarita, L. (2009). McKinney-Vento Homeless Assistance Act Subtitle B – Education for Homeless Children and Youths Program: Turning good law into effective education 2008 update. *Georgetown Journal on Poverty Law & Policy,* 16, 53-98.

Yon, M., Mickelson, R., & Carlton-LaNey, I. (1993). A Child's Place: Developing interagency collaboration on behalf of homeless children. *Education and Urban Society, 25*(4), 410-423.

Yu, M., North, C., LaVesser, P., Osborne, V., and Spitznagel, E. (2008). A comparison study of psychiatric and behavior disorders and cognitive ability among homeless and housed children. *Community Mental Health Journal, 44*(1), 1-10.

Ziesmer, C., Marcoux, L., and Marwell, B. (1994). Homeless children: Are they different from other low-income children? *Social Work, 39*(6), 658-668.

Zima, B. T., Bussing, R., Forness, S. R., and Benjamin, B. (1997). Sheltered homeless children: Their eligibility and unmet need for special education evaluations. *American Journal of Public Health,* 87, 236-240.

Zhang Q., and Sapp D. (2008). A burning issue in teaching: The impact of perceived teacher burnout and nonverbal immediacy on student motivation and affective learning. *Journal of Communication Studies,* 1, 152–168.

Appendix A

Definitions of Homelessness

According to the McKinney-Vento Homeless Assistance Act, "homeless" refers to:

1. An individual or family who lacks a fixed, regular, and adequate nighttime residence;
2. An individual or family with a primary nighttime residence that is a public or private place not designed for or ordinarily used as a regular sleeping accommodation for human beings, including a car, park, abandoned building, bus or train station, airport, or camping ground;
3. An individual or family living in a supervised publicly or privately operated shelter designated to provide temporary living arrangements (including hotels and motels paid for by Federal, State, or local government programs for low-income individuals or by charitable organizations, congregate shelters, and transitional housing);
4. An individual who resided in a shelter or place not meant for human habitation and who is exiting an institution where he or she temporarily resided;
5. An individual or family who:

A. Will imminently lose their housing, including housing they own, rent, or live in without paying rent, are sharing with others, and rooms in hotels or motels not paid for by Federal, State, or local government programs for low-income individuals or by charitable organizations, as evidenced by:

   i. A court order resulting from an eviction action that notifies the individual or family that they must leave within 14 days;

   ii. The individual or family having a primary nighttime residence that is a room in a hotel or motel and where they lack the resources necessary to reside there for more than 14 days; or

   iii. Credible evidence indicating that the owner or renter of the housing will not allow the individual or family to stay for more than 14 days, and any oral statement from an individual or family seeking homeless assistance that is found to be credible shall be considered credible evidence for purposes of this clause;

B. Has no subsequent residence identified; and
C. Lacks the resources or support networks needed to obtain other permanent housing.

6.   Unaccompanied youth and homeless families with children and youth defined as homeless under other Federal statutes who:
A. Have experienced a long term period without living independently in permanent housing;
B. Have experienced persistent instability as measured by frequent moves over such period; and
C. Can be expected to continue in such status for an extended period of time because of chronic disabilities, chronic physical health or mental health conditions, substance addiction, histories of domestic violence or childhood abuse, the presence of a child or youth with a disability, or multiple barriers to employment

While "homeless children and youth" means:
A. Individuals who lack a fixed, regular, and adequate nighttime residence; and (B) includes:
  i. Children and youths who are sharing the housing of other persons due to loss of housing, economic hardship, or a similar reason; are living in motels, hotels, trailer parks, or camping grounds due to the lack of alternative adequate accommodations; are living in emergency or transitional shelters; are abandoned in hospitals; or are awaiting foster care placement.
  ii. Children and youths who have a primary nighttime residence that is a public or private place not designed for or ordinarily used as a regular sleeping accommodation for human beings.
  iii. Children and youths who are living in cars, parks, public spaces, abandoned buildings, substandard housing, bus or train stations, or similar settings.
  iv. Migratory children who qualify as homeless for the purposes of this part because the children are living in circumstances described in clauses (i) through (iii).

The United States Department of Housing and Urban Development defines "homeless" as:

An individual who lacks a fixed, regular, and adequate nighttime residence; as well an individual who has a primary nighttime residence that is a supervised publicly or privately operated shelter designed to provide temporary living accommodations, an institution that provides a temporary residence for individuals intended to be in-stitutionalized; or a public or private place not designed for, or ordinarily used as, a regular sleeping accommodation for human beings.

Appendix B

Text of McKinney-Vento Act (excerpts)

§11431. Statement of policy

The following is the policy of the Congress:

(1) Each State educational agency shall ensure that each child of a homeless individual and each homeless youth has equal access to the same free, appropriate public education, including a public preschool education, as provided to other children and youths.

(2) In any State where compulsory residency requirements or other requirements, in laws, regulations, practices, or policies, may act as a barrier to the identification of, or the enrollment, attendance, or success in school of, homeless children and youths, the State educational agency and local educational agencies in the State will review and undertake steps to revise such laws, regulations, practices, or policies to ensure that homeless children and youths are afforded the same free, appropriate public education as provided to other children and youths.

(3) Homelessness is not sufficient reason to separate students from the mainstream school environment.

(4) Homeless children and youths should have access to the education and other services that such children and youths need to ensure that such children and youths have an opportunity to meet the same challenging State academic standards to which all students are held.

§11432. Grants for State and local activities for the education of homeless children and youths

(a) General authority

The Secretary is authorized to make grants to States in accordance with the provisions of this section to enable such States to carry out the activities described in subsections (d) through (g).

(1) Allocation

(A) Subject to subparagraph (B), the Secretary is authorized to allot to each State an amount that bears the same ratio to the amount appropriated for such year under section 11435 of this title that remains after the Secretary reserves funds under paragraph (2) and uses funds to carry out section 11434(d) and (h) of this title, as the amount allocated under section 1122 of the Elementary and Secondary Education Act of 1965 [20 U.S.C. 6332] to the State for that year bears to the total amount allocated under section 1122 of such Act to all States for that year, except that no State shall receive less than the greater of—

(i) $150,000;

(ii) one-fourth of 1 percent of the amount appropriated under section 11435 of this title for that year; or

(iii) the amount such State received under this section for fiscal year 2001.

(B) If there are insufficient funds in a fiscal year to allot to each State the minimum amount under subparagraph (A), the Secretary shall ratably reduce the allotments to all States based on the proportionate share that each State received under this subsection for the preceding fiscal year.

(d) Activities

Grants under this section shall be used for the following:

(1) To carry out the policies set forth in section 11431 of this title in the State.

(2) To provide services and activities to improve the identification of homeless children and youths (including preschool-aged homeless children) and enable such children and youths to enroll in, attend, and succeed in school, including, if appropriate, in preschool programs.

(3) To establish or designate in the State educational agency an Office of the Coordinator for Education of Homeless Children and Youths that can sufficiently carry out the duties described for the Office in this part in accordance with subsection (f).

(4) To prepare and carry out the State plan described in subsection (g).

(5) To develop and implement professional development programs for liaisons designated under subsection (g)(1)(J)(ii) and other local educational agency personnel—

(A) to improve their identification of homeless children and youths; and

(B) to heighten the awareness of the liaisons and personnel of, and their capacity to respond to, specific needs in the education of homeless children and youths.

(2) Use by State educational agency

A State educational agency may use the grant funds remaining after the State educational agency distributes subgrants under paragraph (1) to conduct activities under subsection (f) directly or through grants or contracts.

(3) Prohibition on segregating homeless students

(A) In general

Except as provided in subparagraph (B) and section 11433(a)(2)(B)(ii) of this title, in providing a free public education to a homeless child or youth, no State receiving funds under this part shall segregate such child or youth in a separate school, or in a separate program within a school, based on such child's or youth's status as homeless.

(B) Exception

Notwithstanding subparagraph (A), paragraphs (1)(J)(i) and (3) of subsection (g), section 11433(a)(2) of this title, and any other provision of this part relating to the placement of homeless children or youths in schools, a State that has a separate school for homeless children or youths that was operated in fiscal year 2000 in a covered county shall be eligible to receive funds under this part for programs carried out in such school if—

(i) the school meets the requirements of subparagraph (C);

(ii) any local educational agency serving a school that the homeless children and youths enrolled in the separate school are eligible to attend meets the requirements of subparagraph (E); and

(iii) the State is otherwise eligible to receive funds under this part.

(C) School requirements

For the State to be eligible under subparagraph (B) to receive funds under this part, the school described in such subparagraph shall—

(i) provide written notice, at the time any child or youth seeks enrollment in such school, and at least twice annually while the child or youth is enrolled in such school, to the parent or guardian of the child or youth (or, in the case of an unaccompanied youth, the youth) that—

(I) shall be signed by the parent or guardian (or, in the case of an unaccompanied youth, the youth);

(II) sets forth the general rights provided under this part;

(III) specifically states—

(aa) the choice of schools homeless children and youths are eligible to attend, as provided in subsection (g)(3)(A);

(bb) that no homeless child or youth is required to attend a separate school for homeless children or youths;

(cc) that homeless children and youths shall be provided comparable services described in subsection (g)(4), including transportation services, educational services, and meals through school meals programs; and

(dd) that homeless children and youths should not be stigmatized by school personnel; and

(IV) provides contact information for the local liaison for homeless children and youths and the State Coordinator for Education of Homeless Children and Youths;

(ii)(I) provide assistance to the parent or guardian of each homeless child or youth (or, in the case of an unaccompanied youth, the youth) to exercise the right to attend the parent's or guardian's (or youth's) choice of schools, as provided in subsection (g)(3)(A); and

(II) coordinate with the local educational agency with jurisdiction for the school selected by the parent or guardian (or youth), to provide transportation and other necessary services;

(iii) ensure that the parent or guardian (or, in the case of an unaccompanied youth, the youth) shall receive the information required by this subparagraph in a manner and form understandable to such parent or guardian (or youth), including, if necessary and to the extent feasible, in the native language of such parent or guardian (or youth); and

(iv) demonstrate in the school's application for funds under this part that such school—

(I) is complying with clauses (i) and (ii); and

(II) is meeting (as of the date of submission of the application) the same Federal and State standards, regulations, and mandates as other public schools in the State (such as complying with section 1111 of the Elementary and Secondary Education Act of 1965 [20 U.S.C. 6311] and providing a full range of education and related services, including services applicable to students with disabilities).

(E) Local educational agency requirements

For the State to be eligible to receive the funds described in subparagraph (B), the local educational agency described in subparagraph (B)(ii) shall—

(i) implement a coordinated system for ensuring that homeless children and youths—

(I) are advised of the choice of schools provided in subsection (g)(3)(A);

(II) are immediately enrolled, in accordance with subsection (g)(3)(C), in the school selected under subsection (g)(3)(A); and

(III) are promptly provided necessary services described in subsection (g)(4), including transportation, to allow homeless children and youths to exercise their choices of schools under subsection (g)(3)(A);

(ii) document that written notice has been provided—

(I) in accordance with subparagraph (C)(i) for each child or youth enrolled in a separate school under subparagraph (B); and

(II) in accordance with subsection (g)(6)(A)(vi);

(iii) prohibit schools within the agency's jurisdiction from referring homeless children or youths to, or requiring homeless children and youths to enroll in or attend, a separate school described in subparagraph (B);

(iv) identify and remove any barriers that exist in schools within the agency's jurisdiction that may have contributed to the creation or existence of separate schools described in subparagraph (B); and

(v) not use funds received under this part to establish—

(I) new or additional separate schools for homeless children or youths; or

(II) new or additional sites for separate schools for homeless children or youths, other than the sites occupied by the schools described in subparagraph (B) in fiscal year 2000.

(f) Functions of the Office of the Coordinator

The Coordinator for Education of Homeless Children and Youths established in each State shall—

(1) gather and make publicly available reliable, valid, and comprehensive information on—

(A) the number of homeless children and youths identified in the State, which shall be posted annually on the State educational agency's website;

(B) the nature and extent of the problems homeless children and youths have in gaining access to public preschool programs and to public elementary schools and secondary schools;

(C) the difficulties in identifying the special needs and barriers to the participation and achievement of such children and youths;

(D) any progress made by the State educational agency and local educational agencies in the State in addressing such problems and difficulties; and

(E) the success of the programs under this part in identifying homeless children and youths and allowing such children and youths to enroll in, attend, and succeed in, school;

(2) develop and carry out the State plan described in subsection (g);

(3) collect data for and transmit to the Secretary, at such time and in such manner as the Secretary may reasonably require, a report containing information necessary to assess the educational needs of homeless children and youths within the State, including data necessary for the Secretary to fulfill the responsibilities under section 11434(h) of this title;

(4) in order to improve the provision of comprehensive education and related services to homeless children and youths and their families, coordinate activities and collaborate with—

(A) educators, including teachers, special education personnel, administrators, and child development and preschool program personnel;

(B) providers of services to homeless children and youths and their families, including public and private child welfare and social services agencies, law enforcement agencies, juvenile and family courts, agencies providing mental health services, domestic violence agencies, child care providers, runaway and homeless youth centers, and providers of services and programs funded under the Runaway and Homeless Youth Act (42 U.S.C. 5701 et seq.);

(C) providers of emergency, transitional, and permanent housing to homeless children and youths, and their families, including public housing agencies, shelter operators, operators of transitional housing facilities, and providers of transitional living programs for homeless youths;

(D) local educational agency liaisons designated under subsection (g)(1)(J)(ii) for homeless children and youths; and

(E) community organizations and groups representing homeless children and youths and their families;

(5) provide technical assistance to and conduct monitoring of local educational agen-

cies in coordination with local educational agency liaisons designated under subsection (g)(1)(J)(ii), to ensure that local educational agencies comply with the requirements of subsection (e)(3) and paragraphs (3) through (7) of subsection (g);

(6) provide professional development opportunities for local educational agency personnel and the local educational agency liaison designated under subsection (g)(1) (J)(ii) to assist such personnel and liaison in identifying and meeting the needs of homeless children and youths, and provide training on the definitions of terms related to homelessness specified in sections 11302, 11360, and 11434a of this title to the liaison; and

(7) respond to inquiries from parents and guardians of homeless children and youths, and (in the case of unaccompanied youths) such youths, to ensure that each child or youth who is the subject of such an inquiry receives the full protections and services provided by this part.

(3) Local educational agency requirements

(A) In general

The local educational agency serving each child or youth to be assisted under this part shall, according to the child's or youth's best interest—

(i) continue the child's or youth's education in the school of origin for the duration of homelessness—

(I) in any case in which a family becomes homeless between academic years or during an academic year; and

(II) for the remainder of the academic year, if the child or youth becomes permanently housed during an academic year; or

(ii) enroll the child or youth in any public school that nonhomeless students who live in the attendance area in which the child or youth is actually living are eligible to attend.

(B) School stability

In determining the best interest of the child or youth under subparagraph (A), the local educational agency shall—

(i) presume that keeping the child or youth in the school of origin is in the child's or youth's best interest, except when doing so is contrary to the request of the child's or youth's parent or guardian, or (in the case of an unaccompanied youth) the youth;

(ii) consider student-centered factors related to the child's or youth's best interest, including factors related to the impact of mobility on achievement, education, health, and safety of homeless children and youth, giving priority to the request of the child's or youth's parent or guardian or (in the case of an unaccompanied youth) the youth;

(iii) if, after conducting the best interest determination based on consideration of the presumption in clause (i) and the student-centered factors in clause (ii), the local educational agency determines that it is not in the child's or youth's best interest to attend the school of origin or the school requested by the parent or guardian, or (in the case of an unaccompanied youth) the youth, provide the child's or youth's parent or guardian or the unaccompanied youth with a written explanation of the reasons for its determination, in a manner and form understandable to such parent, guardian, or unaccompanied youth, including information regarding the right to appeal under subparagraph (E); and

(iv) in the case of an unaccompanied youth, ensure that the local educational agency liaison designated under paragraph (1)(J)(ii) assists in placement or enrollment decisions under this subparagraph, gives priority to the views of such unaccompanied youth, and provides notice to such youth of the right to appeal under subparagraph (E).

(C) Immediate enrollment

(i) In general

The school selected in accordance with this paragraph shall immediately enroll the homeless child or youth, even if the child or youth—

(I) is unable to produce records normally required for enrollment, such as previous academic records, records of immunization and other required health records, proof of residency, or other documentation; or

(II) has missed application or enrollment deadlines during any period of homelessness.

(ii) Relevant academic records

The enrolling school shall immediately contact the school last attended by the child or youth to obtain relevant academic and other records.

(iii) Relevant health records

If the child or youth needs to obtain immunizations or other required health records, the enrolling school shall immediately refer the parent or guardian of the child or youth, or (in the case of an unaccompanied youth) the youth, to the local educational agency liaison designated under paragraph (1)(J)(ii), who shall assist in obtaining necessary immunizations or screenings, or immunization or other required health records, in accordance with subparagraph (D).

(D) Records

Any record ordinarily kept by the school, including immunization or other required health records, academic records, birth certificates, guardianship records, and evaluations for special services or programs, regarding each homeless child or youth shall be maintained—

(i) so that the records involved are available, in a timely fashion, when a child or youth enters a new school or school district; and

(ii) in a manner consistent with section 1232g of title 20.

(E) Enrollment disputes

If a dispute arises over eligibility, or school selection or enrollment in a school—

(i) the child or youth shall be immediately enrolled in the school in which enrollment is sought, pending final resolution of the dispute, including all available appeals;

(ii) the parent or guardian of the child or youth or (in the case of an unaccompanied youth) the youth shall be provided with a written explanation of any decisions related to school selection or enrollment made by the school, the local educational agency, or the State educational agency involved, including the rights of the parent, guardian, or unaccompanied youth to appeal such decisions;

(iii) the parent, guardian, or unaccompanied youth shall be referred to the local educational agency liaison designated under paragraph (1)(J)(ii), who shall carry out the dispute resolution process as described in paragraph (1)(C) as expeditiously as possible after receiving notice of the dispute; and

(iv) in the case of an unaccompanied youth, the liaison shall ensure that the youth is immediately enrolled in the school in which the youth seeks enrollment pending resolution of such dispute.

(F) Placement choice

The choice regarding placement shall be made regardless of whether the child or youth lives with the homeless parents or has been temporarily placed elsewhere.

(G) Privacy

Information about a homeless child's or youth's living situation shall be treated as a student education record, and shall not be deemed to be directory information, under section 1232g of title 20.

(H) Contact information

Nothing in this part shall prohibit a local educational agency from requiring a parent or guardian of a homeless child or youth to submit contact information.

(I) School of origin defined

In this paragraph:

(i) In general

The term "school of origin" means the school that a child or youth attended when permanently housed or the school in which the child or youth was last enrolled, including a preschool.

(ii) Receiving school

When the child or youth completes the final grade level served by the school of origin, as described in clause (i), the term "school of origin" shall include the designated receiving school at the next grade level for all feeder schools.

(4) Comparable services

Each homeless child or youth to be assisted under this part shall be provided services comparable to services offered to other students in the school selected under paragraph (3), including the following:

(A) Transportation services.

(B) Educational services for which the child or youth meets the eligibility criteria, such as services provided under title I of the Elementary and Secondary Education Act of 1965 (20 U.S.C. 6301 et seq.) or similar State or local programs, educational programs for children with disabilities, and educational programs for English learners.

(C) Programs in career and technical education.

(D) Programs for gifted and talented students.

(E) School nutrition programs.

(6) Local educational agency liaison

(A) Duties

Each local educational agency liaison for homeless children and youths, designated under paragraph (1)(J)(ii), shall ensure that—

(i) homeless children and youths are identified by school personnel through outreach and coordination activities with other entities and agencies;

(ii) homeless children and youths are enrolled in, and have a full and equal opportunity to succeed in, schools of that local educational agency;

(iii) homeless families and homeless children and youths have access to and receive educational services for which such families, children, and youths are eligible, including services through Head Start programs (including Early Head Start programs) under the Head Start Act (42 U.S.C. 9831 et seq.), early intervention services under part C of the Individuals with Disabilities Education Act (20 U.S.C. 1431 et seq.), and other preschool programs administered by the local educational agency;

(iv) homeless families and homeless children and youths receive referrals to health care services, dental services, mental health and substance abuse services, housing services, and other appropriate services;

(v) the parents or guardians of homeless children and youths are informed of the educational and related opportunities available to their children and are provided with meaningful opportunities to participate in the education of their children;

(vi) public notice of the educational rights of homeless children and youths is disseminated in locations frequented by parents or guardians of such children and youths, and unaccompanied youths, including schools, shelters, public libraries, and soup kitchens, in a manner and form understandable to the parents and guardians of homeless children and youths, and unaccompanied youths;

(vii) enrollment disputes are mediated in accordance with paragraph (3)(E);

(viii) the parent or guardian of a homeless child or youth, and any unaccompanied youth, is fully informed of all transportation services, including transportation to the school of origin, as described in paragraph (1)(J)(iii), and is assisted in accessing transportation to the school that is selected under paragraph (3)(A);

(ix) school personnel providing services under this part receive professional development and other support; and

(x) unaccompanied youths—

(I) are enrolled in school;

(II) have opportunities to meet the same challenging State academic standards as the State establishes for other children and youth, including through implementation of the procedures under paragraph (1)(F)(ii); and

(III) are informed of their status as independent students under section 1087vv of title 20 and that the youths may obtain assistance from the local educational agency liaison to receive verification of such status for purposes of the Free Application for Federal Student Aid described in section 1090 of title 20.

(B) Notice

State Coordinators established under subsection (d)(3) and local educational agencies shall inform school personnel, service providers, advocates working with homeless families, parents and guardians of homeless children and youths, and homeless children and youths of the duties of the local educational agency liaisons, and publish an annually updated list of the liaisons on the State educational agency's website.

(D) Homeless status

A local educational agency liaison designated under paragraph (1)(J)(ii) who receives training described in subsection (f)(6) may affirm, without further agency action by the Department of Housing and Urban Development, that a child or youth who is eligible for and participating in a program provided by the local educational agency, or the immediate family of such a child or youth, who meets the eligibility requirements of this chapter for a program or service authorized under subchapter IV, is eligible for such program or service.